Compo-Lit!
FRENCH LITERATURE
ESSAY-WRITING

Also by Rod Hares

Teaching French
Der deutsche Aufsatz (with C.G. Clemmetsen)
Compo! (with Geneviève Elliott)

To the brave people of Mount Macedon, Victoria, Australia, in admiration of their courage and determination during the bushfire disasters of 1983.

COMPO-LIT!

FRENCH LITERATURE
ESSAY-WRITING

ROD HARES

HODDER AND STOUGHTON

LONDON SYDNEY AUCKLAND TORONTO

Hares, R.J.
  Compo-lit!
  1. French language——Composition and exercises
  I. Title
  808'.0441   PC2410
  ISBN 0 340 34451 2

First published 1984
Third impression 1985

Type Set by Butler & Tanner Ltd, Frome and London

Printed in Great Britain for
Hodder and Stoughton Educational,
a division of Hodder and Stoughton Ltd
Mill Road, Dunton Green, Sevenoaks, Kent
by Richard Clay (The Chaucer Press) Ltd, Bungay, Suffolk.

Contents

Acknowledgements

Thanks are due to the following for their kind help:

My wife Lyn, for her patient reading of the proofs.

Miss Kaye Smith (VIth Form, Rufford Comprehensive School, Edwinstowe, Notts) for the essay on Bazin on page 120.

Mr Bill Price (former Head of Modern Languages, Bridgend Boys' Grammar School) for the Poetry Check-List on page 71 and for his teaching.

Dr Michael Spencer (former Lecturer in French, Sydney Sussex College, Cambridge) for his encouragement of a callow student.

Mr Tony White (formerly Senior Lecturer in English and Drama, Northumberland College) for his inspirational drama-teaching and for his wisdom.

Mr Mel Cox, French Department, and Mr Graham Durban, German Department, Rufford School, for their useful observations and support.

Mr David Carter, Mr Ray Halliday, Mr Leslie Banks for some question material.

As always, special thanks to Miss Helen Hancock of Hodder and Stoughton for her help and encouragement.

Rod Hares

For permission to quote copyright material the editors and publishers wish to thank: The Radio Times for extracts on pages 111, 112 and 113; The Times Newspapers Ltd for 1) 'Escaping the Octopus' by Gillian Tindall and 2) 'The Transformation of Colette' by Emma Tennant, published in *The Sunday Times* on 18.7.82 and 6.9.81.

Foreword

French Literature Essay-Writing is a practical book, meant to help you over practical difficulties. Nonetheless, it would be dishonest not to admit another reason for writing this manual. I hope that the help you should find within these pages will enable you not only to write more effective literature essays, but also to gain greater enjoyment of your reading. A good book, like a good friend, is a companion to stay with us in times of trouble and to regale our spirits in times of happiness. May I wish you success in your writing and much joy in your reading!

Rod Hares,
December 1982

1

What is a French 'Literature' Essay?

What is a French 'literature' essay? This is a good question to ask yourself. A thoughtful answer will help you to achieve a sound approach to advanced essay-writing as part of the study of French literature. To find out exactly what the literature essay is, let us look at some of the more common traps into which students may fall, and which can be quite easily avoided. As a start, compare these short pieces written by two different individuals on the same essay topic

(a) Étienne does not get on as well with his mother, Marion, as he used to, although he seems to be very close to her. They disagree at breakfast and at many other times. He does not do as she suggests and when he finds out that his father was a murderer, he shuts himself away in the library and looks through all the reports of his father's trial. Étienne decides he is just like his father and sets out to become a notorious criminal by killing Maxime Joubert, the new man in his mother's life, of whom he is very jealous.

   He does not manage to do this, although he tries quite hard after listening to M. Thuillier, his philosophy teacher, and eventually he decides that perhaps his mother was right after all and that M. Joubert was not such a bad man. He is much happier at the end of the story than at the beginning.

(b) The major concern of the novel is with Étienne's psychological and spiritual development from his initial position as a highly intelligent but insecure adolescent through a sharp personal crisis to the beginnings of adulthood. The personal crisis is precipitated by the knowledge that his dead father was an infamous murderer. Étienne's mother's apparent rejection of him for Maxime Joubert, whose excellent qualities Étienne chooses to ignore, is sufficient to allow him to identify temporarily with the recognizably evil side of his father, since this will allow him to punish both himself and his mother.

   Étienne proceeds to a low point in his personal despair through encounters with Thuillier, who is his philosophy teacher, and with Maxime, who represent respectively the evil and the good sides of human nature. Good triumphs eventually, despite the abortive attempt to kill Maxime. Such a triumph is brought about by a combination of Étienne's underlying reliability and the basic good influence of his mother. These have been built up over the years and are sufficiently strong to overcome a short-lived crisis brought about by the pressures of growing-up.

Before you are given any more hints, you will have seen some of the lessons for yourself. Example (a) rambles aimlessly and does little but tell the story of the work, with no attempt at analysis. Example (b) shows that the writer has set out to look beneath the surface of the tale.

The key-words are *story-telling* and *analysis*. The former is the most common fault found in literature essays and the latter is precisely what is required. If, before you start writing on a theme, you can discipline yourself not to fall into the trap of giving a potted account of the events in the story, when what you are required to do is to *interpret* those events, you will have made a good beginning to your literary career.

Apart from the smoother style of example (b), which we shall leave for the moment, what is there about it which is *analytical* and makes it more worth reading than (a)? We can find this out by making a list of the specific points which show that the writer has sifted below the immediate surface of the novel. These are:

1 *The major concern . . . sharp personal crisis.* The essayist has looked for and found the basic theme of the work.
2 *The personal . . . murderer* indicates that the writer has realized the function of Étienne's discovery that his father has been a mass murderer. The discovery is not simply an occurrence, but becomes a hub on which later events turn.
3 *Étienne's mother's apparent rejection . . .* the insertion of *apparent* makes it clear that the essayist realizes that at no time has Étienne been truly rejected by Marion.
4 *since this will allow him . . .* reveals an understanding of the basic psychology of relationships.
5 *who represent the evil and the good sides of human nature* shows that the writer understands Troyat's use of straightforward symbolical characters.
6 *Such a triumph . . . of growing-up* shows a good understanding of the way in which Troyat has built up his characters and their interaction and of the internal structure of the novel.

This model, unlike the first example, attempts to interpret the work for the person reading the essay. Interpretation is, of course, closely related to analysis and to achieve this style of writing, you will find it helpful to write for your reader, as if he or she did not know the book and you were guiding them through the author's intentions without retelling the story.

If, you may well ask, you are expected to avoid telling the story of the book you are reading but are expected to be able to provide analysis, how precisely are you meant to achieve this?

Start by trying to view the work objectively, that is, by trying not to be too emotional in your reaction, and by attempting to look beneath the story line, so that you can see what is going on below. This is not easy. In fact, it can be very difficult, since books we read often produce a strong emotional response in us. However, a powerful reaction to a work can be put to good use. Ask yourself *why* you like the book so much, or feel angry at a specific character's behaviour or are greatly saddened by a particular event. Even at this early stage, a basic lesson is emerging.

If you can ask yourself not *what* happens, but *why* it happens, then you will have made an important early step towards a successful understanding of the work.

In order to help yourself to do this, you should understand that there are several basic processes operating in the complex relationship between a work and its reader. Among these processes, there are two vital ones which have not changed since they were identified by Classical Greek men of letters in the early days of literature. They are called *catharsis* and *vicarious action*.

CATHARSIS

Strictly speaking, the word *catharsis* means a purging of the emotions and derives from early Greek theatre, where drama was seen to serve the highly useful civic function of allowing audiences to give vent to potentially anti-social feelings such as anger, frustration, greed, violence. It was felt the citizens would return home contented after a visit to the theatre, their excess emotions drained, and in consequence, were more likely to remain calm and rational in their daily life.

Whatever the social benefits of drama, be it in Periclean Athens or down-town New York, the phenomenon known as catharsis will always function in a play or a work for reading, such as a novel or short story, provided the material is sufficiently gripping to involve the audience or readership to the extent that they feel taken out of themselves and identify with the characters and the events taking place.

An often-quoted example of the way in which a skilful craftsman can manipulate his audience into a strong personal involvement is reputed to have occurred during a performance of Shakespeare's *Othello* at Stratford. Once, when the play had reached the point where Othello was smothering Desdemona for apparently having been unfaithful to him with Iago, a member of the audience is said to have got up from his seat and shouted, 'Stop it, you fool! Can't you see she's innocent?'

This is a classic example of how a high emotional charge is generated in a person observing a fictional drama as it unfolds. The man concerned had become so involved that his emotions had crossed the line between fiction and reality. Catharsis is the drawing off of this emotional charge. It is something that we will often have experienced as we leave the cinema or switch off the television and find ourselves drained by the events we have watched.

The following passage from Marcel Proust's *Du Côté de chez Swann* is a good example of the way in which the high emotional charge of the writing may transfer itself to the reader, who, like the young Marcel in the book, is granted the position of the voyeur, spying on an unpleasant situation with both sadistic and pathetic undertones:

(Marcel has spied on Mlle. Vinteuil and her dominant woman friend, who play out a ritual before the latter spits on the photograph of the dead M. Vinteuil)
 – Je n'oserais pas cracher dessus? sur *ça*? dit l'amie avec une brutalité voulue.
  Je n'entendis pas davantage, car Mlle. Vinteuil, d'un air las, gauche, affairé, honnête

et triste, vint fermer les volets et la fenêtre, mais je savais maintenant, pour toutes les souffrances que pendant sa vie M. Vinteuil avait supportées à cause de sa fille, ce qu'après la mort il avait reçu d'elle en salaire.

Having read this short extract, try to answer the following questions, giving reasons for your answers:

1 Do you feel negatively towards Mlle. Vinteuil and her friend? If so, what emotions has she aroused and why?
2 What do you feel is Proust's attitude to the scene depicted? Is it directly stated, or do we gather it by implication?
3 What do you think are the feelings of the young Marcel?

VICARIOUS ACTION OR INVOLVEMENT

The term *vicarious* is defined in the dictionary as *acting or doing for another*.

We have already seen how, when we read a good fictional work or follow a play of similar quality, a complex process develops. We become so immersed in events, at least for short periods of time, that we feel with or against the characters to the extent that the story might actually be taking place. We have accepted that our emotional response creates a form of catharsis, whereby our highly charged feelings are purged and we may even feel some conscious relief as a result of this process.

Vicarious involvement may be termed a form of *self-substitution* and occurs when our cathartic response to a work is strong enough for us to want to step inside the printed page and to become one of the characters. This is a most complex process, since we will often be totally unaware that it is happening.

Yet, most of us are cathartically involved almost every day of our lives, so much do we live off other people's experience as well as our own. All of us have our favourite works of fiction, plays, films, theatre, radio and television stories in which, at times, we will have identified so closely with one of the characters or with what (s)he is doing, that we might almost as well have been committing his or her actions ourselves. We will have *substituted* ourselves for that character. For a few moments, we may have been the heroic figure in a tale of action, the beautiful woman casting a spell over those with whom she comes into contact, the millionaire spending his money so liberally, the recluse scientist working for humanity, the great philanthropist. Something inside us has wanted to pass over the barrier which separates us from the fictional character and we have substituted ourselves for that person.

However, the process is not always as obvious as in the case of the film buff crashing through the exit doors at the cinema, in the style of James Bond, or gliding demurely down the staircase, trailing shades of Scarlett O'Hara, the provocative heroine of *Gone With The Wind*.

There is a more common half-way position in which we may not actually become the characters who people the fictional world, but in which we identify very closely with some of their actions. In other words there is a degree of selectivity about our self-substitution.

Perhaps the best way to think of this is to be aware of the fact that readers are normally in the position of observers at the window. They are privileged to watch all that is going on, without ever being seen by the participants. From time to time the observers will be so touched by the events that, without entering into the personality of the characters, they will still feel as if they themselves are perpetrating some of the fictionalized actions.

In *La Condition humaine*, for example (see page 11), although they may not see themselves as Tchen, they may nonetheless feel themselves hurling the bomb at the car of the Chinese military dictator. This will happen, precisely because Malraux has drawn such a sympathetic picture of Tchen and such a desperate one of the conditions in which he lives, that they sympathize with his actions and empathize with him.

Note what has happened. By skilful writing, the author has manipulated the reader into vicarious participation in deeds which in real life (s)he would not contemplate.

Thus, the writer's craft is partly one of manipulation, whereby the reader becomes an accomplice in a series of fictionalized actions. The better the writer, the better the manipulation. In any work that you study, ask yourself these fundamental questions:

1 How far does the author succeed in creating life-like characters and a believable world?
2 To what extent does the writer make me suspend my disbelief and allow the environment of the book to become a temporary real world in which I substitute myself from time to time?

DETACHMENT

Although we have considered catharsis and our own vicarious involvement in what we read, we should not look for an emotional charge and high reader involvement in every chapter or scene of a work of art.

The writer does have other purposes. Indeed, his purpose may at times be the opposite and we should look for it. Voltaire, for instance, intent upon opening people's eyes to the need for a change in attitudes, appeals in *Candide* to our faculty of reason, by using humour and other devices to underline the ridiculousness of much of our behaviour and to allow us to stand outside the action. Here, there is little chance of feeling for a while that we are really in Candide's place. The last thing Voltaire wants is that sort of involvement. Instead, he sets out to encourage us into a detached and balanced assessment of the situation. Study the passage below:

> Il plut à monseigneur l'inquisiteur de célébrer un auto-da-fé. Il me fit l'honneur de m'y inviter. Je fus très bien placée; on servit aux dames des rafraîchissements entre la messe et l'exécution. Je fus, à la vérité, saisie d'horreur en voyant brûler ces deux juifs.

Notice how Voltaire situates the tea-party incongruously within the *auto-da-fé* (ceremonial execution). It is so out of place as to be ludicrous. The contrast between the genteel pleasantries indulged in by the people of quality and the violent and squalid surroundings in which they hold their social gathering, leads us to question the executions themselves. By making us smile or laugh at a situation reminiscent of modern black comedy, Voltaire obliges us to employ the reason in our minds. The process is a neat one. We note the imbalance between the two events, think first of all that the tea-party is out of place and continue to the point where we reflect that the executions may be equally inappropriate.

CHARACTER

One of your tasks will often be to assess the author's purpose, which will be at least partly seen through his attitude to his characters. In a short story like Marcel Aymé's 'Les Bottes de sept lieues', his attitude to an anxious mother bringing up her son in hard times may be fairly easily deduced:

> Germaine Buge quitta l'appartement de Mlle. Larrisson, où elle venait de faire deux heures de 'ménage à fond' sous le regard critique de la vieille fille ... Son manteau la protégeait mal ... l'usure l'avait réduit à n'être plus guère qu'une apparence. La bise d'hiver le traversait comme un grillage en fil de fer.

Aymé reflects sympathetically upon Germaine Buge's fragility. She is an anxious woman with considerable burdens and Aymé uses passages such as the above to enlist our compassion.

The author's attitude to his characters and to people in general may be even more directly stated, as in Albert Camus's *La Peste*, where Dr Rieux, who fights tirelessly against the bubonic plague which has struck Oran, is a man to be admired for his commitment to humanity:

> Le docteur Rieux décida alors de rédiger le récit qui s'achève ici, pour ne pas être de ceux qui se taisent, pour témoigner en faveur de ces pestiférés, pour laisser du moins un souvenir de l'injustice et de la violence qui leur avaient été faites, et pour dire simplement ce qu'on apprend au milieu des fléaux, qu'il y a dans les hommes plus de choses à admirer que de choses à mépriser.

You should be aware that the author's attitude to his characters is important, not simply because it shows how he feels about his creations, but also because it will often reveal his purpose in writing the work. A main character may be, like Candide, an honest innocent abroad, undergoing a wide variety of experiences, many of them unpleasant, so that he will eventually mature and symbolize the need for an increasing maturity of judgement in society.

Pierre, the worker-priest in Cesbron's *Les Saints vont en enfer*, is a human-being with his own particular mixture of strengths and weaknesses. He is a character for whom his creator evidently has much affection. The way he behaves and the situations which arise as a consequence of his behaviour suggest that Cesbron views the attempts of the righteous to build a better and more equable society as doomed to failure.

> (Pierre is being removed from his parish in a rough district of Paris, because his activities compromise the Church)
> – Vous agirez comme il vous semblera bon. Je vous éloigne seulement de Sagny, et pour

des raisons tout à fait matérielles. Et ..." Son regard finissait la phrase: "... et j'ai peut-être tort."

By contrast, Flaubert's Emma Bovary represents a certain type of articulate woman emerging in later nineteenth-century society and stultified by a lack of spiritual and intellectual contact. It is an interesting historical reflection to note that one of the major reasons why *Madame Bovary* caused such a scandal was that Flaubert failed to condemn his main character entirely. It is evident from the book that he had a certain sympathy with her, despite the fact that she decided to do away with her husband.

> Ce qui l'exaspérait, c'est que Charles n'avait pas l'air de se douter de son supplice. La conviction où il était de la rendre heureuse lui semblait une insulte imbécile et sa sécurité là-dessus, de l'ingratitude.
> (Charles's very obtuseness and lack of imagination are suggested to be prime factors in his wife's disenchantment. Flaubert builds up a case whereby it is their very incompatibility which is a major cause of Emma's wayward behaviour. It is insufficient to indict her as a wanton woman, Charles shares the responsibility for her later demise.)

ASSIGNMENTS

1 Choose a character from a French work and try to show what the author thinks of her/him.
2 Select a character from a book you have read and show how (s)he fits in with the author's purpose.

Often, an author's attitude to his characters will not be especially clear, since he will wish not to intrude, so do not expect to be able to deduce his reactions. Instead, concentrate on asking yourself how *you* feel about the characters. Think of a character in one of your set books and try to find 4–6 examples in the text to show why you feel one of the following emotions towards him/her:

affection/dislike/sympathy/scorn/pride/resentment/envy/disbelief/anger/amusement/derision/disgust.

Character analysis is dealt with in full in Chapter 6, but, for the moment, it may be helpful to refer to the character-profile check-list on page 46.

ATMOSPHERE

Another key factor which needs to be taken into account is the prevailing atmosphere within the book. This will give you a good indication of some of the author's reasons for writing.

In *La Tête sur les épaules* the atmosphere is often tense, much of the action takes place in the mind, and there is a hermetic, shut-in quality about the scenes. The ambiance which results is well-suited to a short novel which has as its subject a late adolescent undergoing a powerful intellectual crisis, during which his own sanity is brought into question:

Il se trouva seul et désoeuvré dans l'antichambre où une glace brillait entre les fantômes de deux manteaux parallèles. Le bruit de la machine à coudre devint assourdissant. Puis il y eut un silence: Mme. Marthe coupait le fil, faisait pivoter l'étoffe. Quand la machine à coudre se remit en marche, Étienne eut l'impression qu'une aiguille rapide le perçait, lui-même de mille trous.

Even the part of the house in which his mother's dressmaking business is carried out seems at times to pose a threat to him.

Whenever you have to assess the prevailing atmosphere within the work you are studying, use the check-list below to help you:

ATMOSPHERE

Place a tick in the box opposite each adjective you feel describes the atmosphere of the book in question:

Quality	√	*Page Ref.*		√	*Page Ref.*
affectionate			insecure		
anxious			lacking feeling		
calm			morbid		
claustrophobic			optimistic		
coarse			passionate		
dead			pessimistic		
despairing			petty		
dramatic			relaxed		
empty			relieved		
energetic			resentful		
exuberant			reverential		
farcical			sad		
forbidding			scandalous		
gay			secure		
glamorous			serious		
guilt-ridden			sinister		
happy			slow		
hopeful			soporific		
humble			soulless		
humorous			sophisticated		
inert			tense		
innocent			tragic		
			violent		
Additions:			warm		

ASSIGNMENTS

3 Study each short passage and choose from the alternatives what sort of atmosphere you think is being built up. Give reasons for your decision.

(a) (*Les Saints vont en enfer*)

– Tu trouveras ça dans tout Sagny,* dit Bernard: des impasses qui communiquent avec la rue par un couloir ou par une grille. Des maisons basses, pas d'étages ou un seul, divisées en chambres.

impoverished/confused/harmonious/dis-united

(b) (*Thérèse Desqueyroux*)

Les deux hommes, un instant, observèrent la jeune femme immobile, serrée dans son manteau, et ce blême visage qui n'exprimait rien. . . . Ils traversèrent la place: des feuilles de platane étaient collées aux bancs trempés de pluie.

lively/provincial/grey/optimistic

(c) (*Germinal*)

Le mineur acheva d'un geste. Son tour était arrivé, la cage avait reparu, de son mouvement aisé et sans fatigue. Il s'y accroupit avec des camarades, elle replongea, puis jaillit de nouveau au bout de quatre minutes à peine, pour engloutir une autre charge d'hommes.

warm and promising/far-fetched/impersonal/frenzied

(d) (*Menuet* from Maupassant's *Contes*)

Un parfum de fleurs voltigeait dans les allées proprettes; un bon soleil glissait entre les feuilles et semait sur nous de larges gouttes de lumière. La robe noire de la Castris† semblait toute mouillée de clarté.

musical/harsh/futuristic/evocative

(e) (*Le Chien jaune* – Simenon)

Vendredi 7 Novembre. Concarneau est désert. L'horloge lumineuse de la vieille ville marque onze heures moins cinq. Une tempête du sud-ouest fait s'entrechoquer les barques dans le port. Le vent s'engouffre dans les rues où l'on voit parfois des bouts de papier filer à toute allure au ras du sol.

Quai de l'Aiguillon, il n'y a pas une lumière. Tout est fermé.

forbidding/neutral/small-town/picturesque

(f) (*Germinal*)

Un flot d'or roulait de l'orient à l'occident, sur la plaine immense. Cette chaleur de vie gagnait, s'étendait, en un frisson de jeunesse, où vibraient les soupirs de la terre, le chant des oiseaux, tous les murmures des eaux et des bois. Il faisait bon vivre, le vieux monde voulait vivre un printemps encore.

pessimistic/optimistic/antique/faded

You no doubt noticed that there were two extracts from *Germinal* among the assignments. The two atmospheres evoked are very different from each other and these particular passages were chosen to underline the fact that in a work of any length, there will not necessarily be one, single, ambiance, which remains unchanged from one end of the book to the other.

---

* Sagny is a poor suburb of Paris.
† La Castris – a famous dancer.

THE BACKCLOTH

A related element is the background against which the main events are set. The characters may play out their lives in a city or a small town, in the countryside or at sea, in isolation or in contact with people. They will live in an environment which may be hostile/frenzied/inhospitable/sedate/welcoming/strange/very familiar or many other things.

Whatever its particular quality, it is likely to have a discernible effect on one or more of the main characters in the book. Always try to establish what exactly the effect is of the environment in which individuals find themselves placed.

If the influence is sufficiently strong to determine almost from birth the way in which a character behaves, as for instance in many of Maupassant's *contes* or Zola's novels, then the author's approach is said to be deterministic, i.e. the character's behaviour is *determined* by his or her surroundings. A very clear example is the way in which Maupassant, in *Un Bandit Corse*, uses the uncomprisingly harsh environment of part of Corsica, to explain the similar behaviour of its sons. When a young man by the name of Sainte-Lucie, who is apparently mild to the point of self-effacement, eventually invokes the vendetta, kills and becomes the most ferocious bandit Corsica has known, the roots of his behaviour are there to see in the searing sun and the impassively cruel rock landscape:

> Bientôt nous fûmes au fond de ce trou sauvage et d'une inimaginable beauté.
>
> Pas une herbe, pas une plante; du granit, rien que du granit. À perte de vue devant nous, un désert de granit étincelant, chauffé comme un four par un furieux soleil qui semble exprès suspendu au-dessus de cette gorge de pierre.

Mostly, the relationship between the backcloth and the development of character will not be quite so strong, though it may be just as effective. In *La Tête sur les épaules*, given the fact that Étienne is an adolescent struggling towards adulthood and lives alone with his attractive widowed mother in a flat above her dressmaking business, what do you feel to be the significance of the following description of the house and its atmosphere?

> Le babillage idiot de la machine à coudre faisait trembler le parquet. Mme. Marthe et Mlle. Suzanne travaillaient là, dans un désordre d'étoffes déchiquetées, de bobines, de ciseaux et de journaux de mode. Les chapeaux de ces dames étaient posés sur la cheminée, de part et d'autre d'une pendule en métal jaune à colonnettes de marbre.
>
> (See also page 53.)

The passage emphasizes the femininity and the somewhat oppressive, isolated nature of the house. It is hardly surprising that Étienne is about to break away from its restrictions.

If we stay for a moment with the theme of the adolescent developing into the emerging adult, we will see the same kind of relationship between backcloth and future action in *Le Grand Meaulnes*, where the limitations of the school background clash with the glamorous glimpses Meaulnes has caught of what he thinks is adult life. The discord between the two environments is symbolized by the way in which Meaulnes, once he has returned from his adventure in the outside world, is ostracized by the other scholars, and Seurel with him:

Rien ne nous rappelait l'aventure de Meaulnes sinon ce fait étrange que depuis l'après-midi 'de son' retour nous n'avions plus d'amis. Aux récréations, les mêmes jeux qu'autrefois s'organisaient, mais Jasmin ne parlait jamais plus au grand Meaulnes. Les soirs, aussitôt la classe balayée, la cour se vidait comme au temps où j'étais seul, et je voyais errer mon compagnon, du jardin au hangar et de la cour à la salle à manger.
    (See also page 80.)

The backcloth can be equally reassuring for other individuals. Elsewhere in the same book, both before and after Meaulnes' presence, Seurel is seen to find security of a sort in the schoolroom and related locales.

Meaulnes parti, je n'étais plus son compagnon d'aventures, le frère de ce chasseur de pistes; je redevenais un gamin du bourg pareil aux autres. Et cela était facile et je n'avais qu'à suivre pour cela mon inclination la plus naturelle.

ASSIGNMENTS

4 Study each of the following short extracts and try to assess the relationship between backcloth and character.

(a) *Les Saints vont en enfer*
La grève fut décidée; Henri donna son nom le lendemain; le lundi, les trois quarts des entreprises de Sagny se trouvaient en grève. Pierre et Madeleine furent chargés du comité de solidarité. . . . Les prêtres-ouvriers qui se retrouvèrent à la Mission, le mardi suivant, étaient presque tous en grève. Ils comparèrent leurs bulletins de paye en silence.

What does the worker-priests' reaction to the backcloth tell us about them, as people?

(b) *Antigone*
Il faut pourtant qu'il y en ait qui disent oui (à la responsabilité). Il faut pourtant qu'il y en ait qui mènent la barque. Cela prend l'eau de toutes parts, c'est plein de crimes, de bêtise, de misère . . . Et le gouvernement est là qui ballotte. L'équipage ne veut plus rien faire.
What do you learn about Créon from his description of the social chaos in Thebes and of his basic role as Head of State?

(c) *La Condition humaine*
La brume, nourrie par la fumée des navires, détruisait peu à peu au fond de l'avenue les trottoirs pas encore vides: des passants affairés y marchaient l'un derrière l'autre, se dépassant rarement, comme si la guerre eût imposé à la ville un ordre tout-puissant. Le silence général de leur marche rendait leur agitation presque fantasque. Ils ne portaient pas de paquets, d'éventaires, ne poussaient pas de petites voitures; cette nuit, il semblait que leur activité n'eût aucun but. Tchen regardait toutes ces ombres qui coulaient sans bruit vers le fleuve, d'un mouvement inexplicable et constant; n'était-ce pas le Destin même, cette force qui les poussaient vers le fond de l'avenue. . . ?
Tchen is on the point of throwing a bomb at Chang-Kai-Shek's car. What does the description of the passers-by and the evening tell you about Tchen and his motivation?

THE HISTORICAL BACKGROUND

Wherever possible, you should take the historical background of the work into account, as this may have a material effect on (a) its subject matter, (b) your interpretation of it.

To prove the point, look at these extracts from (1) Giraudoux's *La Guerre de Troie n'aura pas lieu* (which deals with the impending outbreak of the Trojan War) and (2) Anouilh's *Antigone* (in which the classical Greek heroine refuses to submit to her uncle, Créon, who has become dictator of Athens).

> (1) À la veille de toute guerre, il est courant que deux enfants des peuples en conflit se rencontrent dans quelque innocent village, sur la terrasse au bord d'un lac, dans l'angle d'un jardin.

> (2) Ces temps sont révolus pour Thèbes. Thèbes a droit maintenant à un prince sans histoire.

If you are aware that the first of these plays was written while Europe began to be threatened by the outbreak of the Second World War and the second in 1942, during the German occupation of Paris and a major part of France, then you will realize that the quotations may have a topical reference which it is important to grasp. In (1), for example, Hector and Ulysse are often taken to symbolize Briand and Stresemann, Foreign Secretaries of France and Germany during the late 1920s. *La Guerre de Troie n'aura pas lieu* is more than a sophisticated and somewhat precious re-working of a classical legend, it is a warning of what is to come.

In (2) Anouilh reminds us, as directly as he dares, of the logic that ruthless men use to justify their actions. Whatever else *Antigone* may be, it is a brave play, written by a courageous man. There were many officers from the occupying army sitting in the audience when this play was first put on stage. Some of them must have seen the parallel between Créon's dictatorship and that of Germany.

In each case, the dramatist has chosen to situate his play in classical antiquity and thus to give the action symbolical meaning, since what occurs, despite its apparent remoteness, *symbolizes* current or likely future events, and the universality of human behaviour.

Do not take the '*historical*' in the title of this section too literally, despite the examples above. *Historical* may simply relate to the history of the author, rather than that of the world. So, for *historical*, often read *biographical*. In *Du Côté de chez Swann*, for example, it is important to remember that events in young Marcel's life frequently parallel quite closely those in the childhood of its author, Marcel Proust. When the fictional Marcel says of his mother, that

> la voir fâchée détruisait tout le calme qu'elle m'avait apporté un instant avant

we can be sure that these words mirror quite accurately Proust's own experiences and feelings.

Here, a note of warning should be sounded. Beware the temptation to see characters and events as exact replicas of the author's own past. This is a rare occurrence in fact, since his craft is to *create* out of his own experience.

When you discover parallels between the author's life and the subject-matter of the work, make sure you connect them in your own writing, at least in passing, since awareness of them helps towards a greater understanding of the book.

ASSIGNMENT

5 Study any background notes available on the author of one of your set books. Then, look through the text and try to find at least three passages in which his or her own character and experiences are clearly reflected.

THE STYLE

It is important to be able to assess the implications of the author's style of writing, if you are to achieve a full understanding of the work. The next chapter deals with this in detail.

ASSIGNMENTS

6 Choose a main character from one of your set books and, using short quotations, show how his/her character develops or remains static during the course of the work:

7 Select 4–6 example passages in a book you are studying to illustrate any *one* of the following qualities in a character of your choice:

sympathetic/distant/weak/over-bearing/comic/tragic/violent/irrational/ impulsive/proud/wise/humanitarian/kind/inadequate/anxious/carefree/ evil.

8 Look back at the list of qualities in Assignment 2 and name for each one any character you have encountered who fits the description.

9 Think of an unpleasant character in a set book. Try to locate instances in the text, which show him/her to have redeeming characteristics.

10 Is there any character you have encountered in French literature whose behaviour sometimes seems markedly inconsistent with his/her normal actions? Find example passages in the text to prove your point.

11 Find a character to whom you relate very positively. Give short examples from the text to show why you like him/her.

12 Do the same for a character whom you dislike.

13 Choose a character from a set book, who reminds you of someone you have seen in a film. Make notes on their similarities.

14 Find a character in real life who resembles one of the characters in a French book you have read. Make notes on their similarities.

15 Are you able to find a character in a set book who is simply not true to life? Give 4–6 short examples of his/her behaviour to prove your point.

16 Study the behaviour of a character in a set book and describe where it is typically French.

17 Do you know a work in which any main character resembles the author? Find 3-4 sample passages to support your view.

18 If any main character resembles a famous historical person, find passages in the work which illustrate this similarity.

19 Find any main character who, you feel, fails to come off. Find examples in the text to show why.

20 Find 4-6 example passages in which one of your authors uses physical description to convey character.

21 Is there a conflict between the characters of two of the main protagonists in any of the French books that you have read? If so, find 3-5 points of contrast between the two people.

22 Is there a character in any of your set books who is essentially tragic? Draw examples from the text to show exactly what it is which makes the individual tragic.

2

The Author's Style

What is style, apart from something which is difficult to define? However different writers such as Balzac, Anatole France, Mauriac, Maurois, Colette, Sagan may be, they all have a style of their own. Indeed, it is this very difference which is the essence of the phenomenon we are attempting to define.

Style is an author's personal identifier, his or her set of fingerprints, something characteristic about the way the words have been put down on paper, something so individual and recognizable that a seasoned reader can often identify a writer from a few lines of print he has never seen before.

We ourselves often use the word *style* in a non-literary way, when we say that a person *has style*. What we mean is that the individual we are referring to has something special about him, which marks him out from the crowd, so that we notice him and, even more important, want to notice him, since he brings brightness and life to a scene which may be very run-of-the-mill.

This colloquial definition is not as far removed from the literary implications of the term as it may at first appear. When you are required to analyse an author's style, a good starting point is to ask yourself what it is that is special about the way Butor or Giono writes, what it is which makes them stand out from the crowd of pulp-writers.

By definition, any of the writers you are required to study will have reached the respectability of the A-level study lists, because there is something about them which is special. Apart from the fact that their work will be significant or socially committed or psychologically relevant, it will have an attractiveness, a readability, which draw the literati to it.

The style will be the general feel or texture of what the author writes, but it is difficult to generalize and, fortunately, not necessary here, since we can identify those elements of which an author's style is composed. They are:

1 THE GENERAL QUALITY OF THE WORK

When we read a book simply for pleasure, we do not sift the various elements of style into separate compartments. Rather, we read the story and are left with a general, overall impression of the way the author writes. This should be the starting point for any essay on style. The first question to ask yourself should be *What is my general impression of the way the author writes?* You are likely to decide on one of the following qualities or something similar. The work may be:

optimistic	– throughout, or perhaps despite certain unfortunate events, the author sees hope in the future.
pessimistic	– the over-riding impression is one of gloom. Initiative seems pointless.
epic	– the tale is set in a time or against a background of great events.
small-scale	– the author is concerned with ordinary people from an equally ordinary background. There is no attempt to imply universal significance.
impersonal	– there is little attempt by the writer to intervene or to communicate his or her attitude.
involved	– here, the author intervenes either directly or by allusion.
committed	– events within the narrative arouse our sense of justice or of social conscience, which is the author's main purpose in writing.
celebratory	– there is a feeling of *joie de vivre*, of lightness, spontaneity, rich satisfaction, exultation.
disillusioned	– the work is written in muted tones, with little signs of great bitterness or its opposite. There may be much unpleasant conflict between characters.

ASSIGNMENT

Start an essay on style, by deciding which one or more of the above qualities best represent(s) the feel of any work you have read. Write down the attribute(s) and find 2–4 page references to back up your judgement.

2 NARRATIVE STYLE

Whichever quality you decide is the hallmark of the work, it will have been fostered by the use of one or more of the following narrative styles:

personal	– full of comments which obviously come from the author, or of references to his or her own experience.
detached	– there is no attempt by the author to let his or her feelings intrude.
detailed	– the narrative contains much description, often very painstaking and detailed in its accuracy.
impressionistic	– by contrast, the writer only sketches out the detail or background. A little has to go a long way.
evocative	– details are often vivid enough to conjure up memories in the reader, or to stimulate quite intense feeling.
direct	– the approach is rather matter-of-fact. Detail is given and thoughts are stated in a straightforward manner.
ironic	– the author highlights discrepancies in behaviour or in a situation. What actually occurs is often radically different from professed views or accepted standards of behaviour.

pathetic	– pathos is used to *tug at the reader's heartstrings*. As this cliché implies, it is all too easy for pathos to be overdone and to descend into bathos or sentimentality.
humorous	– significant amounts of humour and comedy may be employed, possibly either as a reflection of the author's attitude to life, or to lighten the implications of a serious message.
serious	– aware of the weight of implications in what (s)he is writing, the author finds little room for humorous distraction.
popular	– this narrative style is not to be confused with the use of humour. Through a wish to communicate directly with a broader readership, the writer may employ a style which sometimes borders on the colloquial. Such a style may also be a reaction to other writers regarded as over-pretentious.
erudite	– the opposite of a popular style, this quality indicates an author who cannot help scattering learned references throughout the text, or using a great deal of intellectual vocabulary and imagery.
loose	– an author is said to have a loose style, when (s)he appears to have written rather carelessly without taking the trouble to link ideas and themes.
tightly constructed	– here, nothing is left to chance, almost every detail seems to be of significance and has to earn its inclusion. The plot and themes are closely and neatly worked through to a precise conclusion.

ASSIGNMENT

As with Section 1, decide which qualities best describe the narrative style of a work you are currently studying. Write them down and, once again, find 2–4 page references to back up your judgement.

3 THE STYLE OF THE LANGUAGE

The style of the language used will inevitably reflect the particular general qualities from those above, which characterize the work. Among the types of expression you will have to identify are:

terse	– this is a clipped style, where no more details or words are used than necessary. Consequently, the narrative moves along very quickly.
prolix	– this is the opposite quality, regarded as a defect. The style is wordy and weighed down with unnecessary detail. The reader may feel impatient with the author.
dense	– this attribute should not be confused with prolixity. Certain authors (most notably, Proust) link ideas and expression closely, often to convey an impression of the complexity of the human relationships which they are attempting to portray.

light	– does not mean superficial. The author employs bright, lively imagery, with touches of humour. The overall effect is often good-humoured, entertaining and likely to make the reader smile with the author and his/her characters, without the need to think too deeply.
lyrical	– the language is carefully chosen in an attempt to create an emotional, usually uplifting response in the reader. In a prose work, such lines will strike you as rather poetic.
prosaic	– the opposite of lyrical, this may be a deliberate device on the part of the author to reflect through the mundane nature of the language and theme, the tediousness of the existences portrayed in the work.
lively	– the author may structure his/her ideas so that the narrative proceeds very rapidly. The style of language may change from character to character and from situation to situation, so that the reader is caught up in a rapid process.
dramatic	– the language is direct and at times even a little exaggerated, to mirror a fast-moving situation, where the reader is involved in great or at least important events.
unstressed	– the author deliberately suppresses emotive language and the narrative proceeds on a monotonous level, often through the use of a standard, almost unvarying sentence pattern.
romantic	– (See the definition of Romanticism on page 144.) This does not simply imply the rosy glow of a tale of love. There may, indeed, be much blood and thunder, or the suggestion of it, provided that the detail never becomes realistic enough to bring us back to the actual world we inhabit.
realistic	– the opposite of romantic. Images and speech are deliberately structured to present a view of life as it is lived. The style may even cause offence through its directness, e.g. by the use of obscene language.

ASSIGNMENTS

1 Decide which adjectives best describe the style of the language used by an author you are studying. Write them down and this time find at least half a dozen page references to back your judgement.

2 In a short chapter, it is impossible to list in detail all the stylistic devices an author might use. We have worked through the broad areas. Now, with the aid of a dictionary and, more important, discussion with your fellow students and teachers, make notes on the following items we have not discussed:

The use of	*Notes*
allegory	
allusion	
anthropomorphism	

antithesis
apostrophe
bathos
contrast
contemporary reference
dramatic irony
ellipsis
historical figures
implication
invective
jargon
listing
oxymoron
parable
sarcasm
symbol

In the course of the next year, try to find at least one example of every one of the above devices in your French reading!

3 For each of the short extracts, answer the multiple-choice question below it. In each case there is only one correct answer.

(a) *Des hommes poussaient, une armée noire, vengeresse, qui germait lentement dans les sillons, grandissant pour les récoltes du siècle futur, et dont la germination allait faire bientôt éclater la terre.*

(E. Zola: Germinal)

The style employed here by Zola is essentially . . .

1 lyrical
2 detached
3 terse
4 erudite

(b) *On a fait sur elle une émission. Jacqueline, trente ans, six enfants. Vit dans une H.L.M. 'coquette' au milieu de terrains vagues, moins coquets. Comment s'en tire-t-elle? Émission féminine. Présence féminine nécessaire; la mienne. Je pose des questions.* (F. Mallet-Joris: *La Maison de papier*)

This quotation is typical of the . . . style of the language.

1 epic
2 prolix
3 popular
4 romantic

(c) *Nous déjeunions tous les matins ensemble, nous dînions, enfin j'étais père, je jouissais de mes enfants. Quand elles étaient rue de la Jussienne, elles ne raisonnaient pas, elles ne savaient rien du monde, elles m'aimaient bien. Mon Dieu! pourquoi ne sont-elles pas toujours restées petites?* (Spoken by an old man close to dying)

(H. de Balzac: *Le Père Goriot*)

Here, Balzac employs ... to evoke the required response.

1 pathos
2 an epic style
3 sarcasm
4 a lyrical style

(d) *L'enfant la suivit. Des renforts de police arrivèrent – trop tard, sans raison. Comme ils passaient devant le café, l'homme en sortit, encadré par les inspecteurs. Sur son passage, les gens s'écartèrent en silence.*

(M. Duras: *Moderato cantabile*)

The style is typically ..., in order that we may concentrate on the action.

1 detailed
2 terse
3 serious
4 loose

(e) *'La paix, c'est d'aimer les autres, pour les obliger à aimer les autres – et ainsi de suite sur toute la terre! Et ce n'est pas facile ...'* ajouta-t-il à mi-voix.

(G. Cesbron: *Les Saints vont en enfer*)

The words of the priest reflect Cesbron's own ... position.

1 impersonal
2 pessimistic
3 detached
4 committed

(f) *On erra cinq jours, six jours dans les lignes, presque sans dormir. On stationnait des heures, des demi-nuits, des demi-jours, en attendant que fussent libres des passages qu'on ne voyait pas.*

(Barbusse: *Le Feu*)

This picture of trench-warfare conveys something of Barbusse's own ... view of the nature of war.

1 epic
2 pessimistic
3 dramatic
4 romantic

(g) *... pour dire simplement ce qu'on apprend au milieu des fléaux, qu'il y a dans les hommes plus de choses à admirer que de choses à mépriser.*

(A. Camus: *La Peste*)

As he concludes his novel, Camus expresses a guarded ... our future.

1 detachment towards
2 involvement in
3 pessimism for
4 optimism for

(h) *Quand du regard il rencontrait sur sa table la photographie d'Odette, ou quand elle venait le voir, il avait peine à identifier la figure de chair ou de bristol avec le trouble douloureux et constant qui habitait en lui.*

(M. Proust: *Du Côté de chez Swann*)

Proust's ... style reflects the way individual personalities and relationships are made up of complex layers.

1 dense
2 prolix
3 celebratory
4 prosaic

(i) (*Juliette apparaît avec un fauteuil d'infirme à roulettes et dossier avec couronnes et insignes royaux.*)

(E. Ionesco: *Le Roi se meurt*, stage directions)

The incongruity of the king's throne being replaced by a wheelchair and a regally decorated back-support underlines Ionesco's ... view of our position.

1 humorous
2 ironic
3 impersonal
4 romantic

(j) *Ulysse: Vous savez ce qui me décide à partir, Hector? ...*
Hector: Je le sais. La noblesse.
Ulysse: Pas précisément. Andromaque a le même battement de cils que Pénélope.

(J. Giraudoux: *La Guerre de Troie n'aura pas lieu*)

Ulysse's revelation that he has decided not to make war on the Trojans because he is reminded of his wife when Andromaque flutters her eyelashes, underlines Giraudoux's ... view of war, its causes and resolutions.

1 evocative
2 humorous
3 serious
4 ironic.

3

Structuring the Essay

The way you structure your essay is crucial both to the impression it will make upon your reader and to its final success. You should not think of an essay's *success* simply in terms of the level of mark it obtains. An essay is a creation which has stemmed from your own brain. Therefore a good composition is an achievement in its own right, of which you should be justifiably proud.

In order for such a work to be worthy of merit, it has to be well-planned and set out, so that those who judge it will be impressed by its clarity and balance. In other words, if there is a clear and logical structure to the essay, your readers will have no trouble in understanding what you are putting forward as a thesis. The material below should help you achieve that sought-after precision.

PLANNING REQUIREMENTS AND RESTRICTIONS

LENGTH

It is difficult to provide anything more than a guideline as to length, but the manageable limits for a non-examination essay would be 3–8 sides of A4, depending on the complexity and scope of the subject. Of this 20–25 per cent might be quotation. In the exam-situation 10–20 per cent quotation is a realistic expectation.

ANSWERING THE QUESTION

The onus is on you to deal specifically with the issue(s) raised in the title. Irrelevant material will not gain credit. Neither will an answer where you decide that the title is not to your taste and substitute a theme of your own choosing. For example, if you have been asked to contrast Créon and Antigone, an analysis of Créon's character alone will not do.

Another typical deviation from the norm is to take a slightly obscure quotation in a title to mean what you want it to mean, so that it will fit in nicely with the material you have prepared (see page 41).

STICKING TO YOUR THEME

This point is dealt with on p. 95 of Chapter 12.

TEXTUAL REFERENCE

When you make general points, try to give specific examples. This will not only show that you know a work reasonably well, but will help the reader see the point you are making (see Chapter 4).

UNDERSTANDING

Your brief is to show that you have understood the implications of the work. It will help you in the structuring of your essay, if, instead of thinking simply about the story-line, you keep reminding yourself of the author's purpose in writing and how (s)he achieves it.

READER INTEREST

It is crucial that you keep in mind the need to interest the person looking at your essay. Even if you feel you do not have any ideas which are startlingly new (and very few people will), you can give your writing a reasonably fresh appearance by varying your vocabulary and the length of your sentences and paragraphs.

Try also to think of some topical event, or of a film or another book, etc, with which you may draw parallels. This all helps to make your reader feel that occasionally something different is being said [see Chapter 14].

MAKING A PLAN

When you are producing the first rough outline of your essay try to find
  (a) 6–8 major points;
  (b) 1–3 textual illustrations of each of these points;
  (c) a suitable order for the points, ending on a strong note;
  (d) other works by your author or by another, with which parallels may be drawn;
  (e) quotations from the text to support your argument.

TYPES OF STRUCTURE

The way an essay is put together is crucial to its success. Something that reads neatly and smoothly will often have the merit of clarity, even though the ideas produced by the writer may be relatively pedestrian. Conversely, an essay will fail to impress despite many potentially perceptive thoughts, if it is so involved and confused that those who read it cannot find their way through it. Thus, the way the essay is structured is just as important as its thought content.

There are several types of structure you may use as a vehicle for your ideas.

1. THE STRONG STRUCTURE

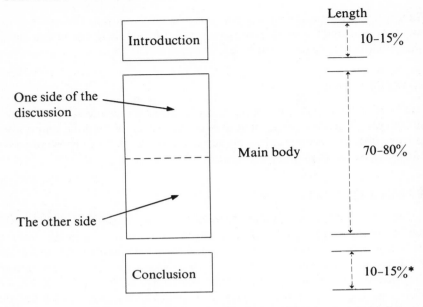

The above diagram is a simple and effective model on which to base the structuring of your essay. It is suitable for many different types of essay topic, since it is straightforward enough to be flexible. If followed closely, it disciplines the essay-writer into a logical approach. The composition is written in three distinct and recognizable sections: an introduction, a main body and a conclusion. Within the argument, the points for either side are kept separate and the stages of development within the essay are signalled to the reader in a series of clear and identifiable steps.

Additionally, if you become accustomed to following such a structure, you will find yourself automatically prepared for the *shape* of your composition, even before you begin writing it. As one of the major problems confronting the essay-writer is often the *shape* of what is being written, such preparation can only be beneficial, especially in the examination situation when the proper organization of available time is so important.

The crux of this structure is the recognition that many types of essay topic, despite their apparent difference, require the writer to discuss two sides of a question and to reach some sort of conclusion as to which side is the stronger. Hence the name, the *strong* structure. If you can break an essay-title down into a requirement for a two-sided discussion and hold back the side which you favour until the second half of your thesis, then you will have created a *strong* position from which to influence the reader.

When the reader reaches the conclusion of the essay, most of what is uppermost in his or her mind will relate to the points most recently read. Presented with a considerable amount of information to read, the human mind quite

* Less in a lengthy essay.

naturally recalls best what it has just processed. Thus, if you, the writer, are attempting to sway the reader towards those arguments you favour, it is advisable to leave these points until the later stages of your composition.

A major difficulty often experienced in writing essays is the fact that it is not always possible to feel very positively about one side of the question. You may feel sufficiently interested in a topic to want to write about it, but your views on the subject may be very mixed. This need not deter you from using an extension of the strong structure, in which you still divide the main body of the essay into two distinct halves but end with no firm commitment to the superiority of one side of the argument.

Suitable topics for the strong structure

Here are some examples of essay topics for which you may use the strong structure, despite their apparent lack of common ground:

(a) A's plays are intrinsically theatrical and do not lend themselves to literary study.

(b) How far do you agree with the statement that X theme is a key to the understanding of Y's work?

(c) What makes B a credible character in C's work?

In (a) you would decide how much of a purely theatrical quality there was in the plays and what exactly there was in the way of literary merit. You would then have to try to decide which took precedence.

Example (b) is perhaps the simplest type of two-sided observation. You decide the extent of your agreement, find what points you can to support each side and order the two sides accordingly. If there is little you can find to support one side of the statement, then the main body of your essay must be one-sided.

Example (c) This is a common type of essay-question, in which you would be well advised not to fall into the trap of absolute agreement. The character will undoubtedly be highly credible, otherwise the title would not have been devised. However, every author is capable of lapses. Check through the text to see if you can find examples of these. There will probably not be many. Still, one or two such instances at the beginning of the main body, will show the reader your astuteness. The points you then make in support of the title will have the weight of authority behind them.

2 THE CHRONOLOGICAL STRUCTURE

This structure is used with essay topics in which you are required to trace a sequence of events or of significant stages. Using a structure in which you list points in the order in which they occur, you will produce an essay which looks something like this:

INTRODUCTION

EVENT/CHANGE/STAGE   A

EVENT/CHANGE/STAGE   B

EVENT/CHANGE/STAGE   C

EVENT/CHANGE/STAGE   D

EVENT/CHANGE/STAGE   E

CONCLUSION

Chronological topics read like the examples below:

(a) Trace the development of the character of Étienne in *La Tête sur les épaules*.
(b) Analyse the stages leading to the *faux dévôt's* downfall in *Le Tartuffe*.
(c) From your reading of Maupassant's short stories, show how his technique can be said to have matured.

Note the key-words *development, stages leading, matured*. They indicate the need to take your points in chronological sequence.

3 THE ROLLING STRUCTURE

This is basically the same type of structure as (2), with the difference that you are not required to take items chronologically. Points A–E (or F) are separate and may roll or flow into each other, but, here, you have the freedom to move as you like within the sequence of the work.

```
┌─────────────────────────────────┐
│ INTRODUCTION                    │
└─────────────────────────────────┘
┌─────────────────────────────────┐
│ DEVICE/THEME/ITEM   A           │
└─────────────────────────────────┘
┌─────────────────────────────────┐
│ DEVICE/THEME/ITEM   B           │
└─────────────────────────────────┘
┌─────────────────────────────────┐
│ DEVICE/THEME/ITEM   C           │
└─────────────────────────────────┘
┌─────────────────────────────────┐
│ DEVICE/THEME/ITEM   D           │
└─────────────────────────────────┘
┌─────────────────────────────────┐
│ DEVICE/THEME/ITEM   E           │
└─────────────────────────────────┘
┌─────────────────────────────────┐
│ DEVICE/THEME/ITEM   F           │
└─────────────────────────────────┘
┌─────────────────────────────────┐
│ DEVICE/THEME/ITEM   G           │
└─────────────────────────────────┘
┌─────────────────────────────────┐
│ DEVICE/THEME/ITEM   H           │
└─────────────────────────────────┘
┌─────────────────────────────────┐
│ CONCLUSION                      │
└─────────────────────────────────┘
```

Types of topic which fit this pattern are:

(a) What devices does Alain-Fournier use to achieve a tense effect in *Le Grand Meaulnes*?
(b) What is the basic theme in Beckett? (Or, analyse the main themes recurrent in the work of Beckett?)
(c) Trace the historical inaccuracies in *La Guerre de Troie n'aura pas lieu*.

4 THE CONTRASTIVE STRUCTURE

Topics in this category are of the *compare and contrast* type, such as:

(a) Compare Mauriac's and Bazin's treatment of the theme of the family in their novels.
(b) In what ways may Rimbaud and Vian both be said to be poets of their time?
(c) Compare and contrast the characters of Maxime Joubert and M. Thuillier in *La Tête sur les épaules*.

Although you may not find it hard to obtain sufficient material to enable you to write on such topics, *contrastives* are a trap for the inexperienced, as the diagram of a typical contrastive essay below will show.

INTRODUCTION

A's quality/reaction/device/attitude, etc.
$\updownarrow$ **compared with** $\updownarrow$
B's quality/reaction/device/attitude, etc.

A's quality/reaction/device/attitude, etc.
$\updownarrow$ **compared with** $\updownarrow$
B's quality/reaction/device/attitude, etc.

A's quality/reaction/device/attitude, etc.
$\updownarrow$ **compared with** $\updownarrow$
B's quality/reaction/device/attitude, etc.

A's quality/reaction/device/attitude, etc.
$\updownarrow$ **compared with** $\updownarrow$
B's quality/reaction/device/attitude, etc.

CONCLUSION

In this type of essay, you are always moving backwards and forwards between A and B, and so you will need to write in a particularly clear and succinct manner to avoid confusing the reader. You may find it easier to use a form of the *strong structure*, i.e. to discuss the various facets of A in the first part of the main-body and then to do the same for B, remarking on the contrasts and comparisons with A as they arise in the second half.

5 THE INTRODUCTION AND THE CONCLUSION

These sections are, of course, common to all the various structures we have looked at, but should not be overlooked simply because they are obvious parts of any essay. Their own internal structures merit as much analysis as the main body.

THE INTRODUCTION

This initial section (of one or two paragraphs and approximately 10 per cent of the total length of the essay) should be exactly what its name implies: it should introduce the reader to the theme. Avoid the temptation to start with a collection of vague sentences which have little to do with the topic.

What steps should you take to ensure that the introduction is direct, relevant and interesting? If the following points can be answered positively, then as far as the thought-content and ideas are concerned, your reader's first reaction is likely to be favourable.

Have you:

1 made at least an oblique reference to the title?
2 presented a list of the main points to come?
3 given some indication of your personal stance?
4 provided a smooth lead-in to the main body?
5 left room for manoeuvre in the conclusion?
6 avoided making your introduction too long/too short?

1 A partial allusion to the title helps to tie you to your theme. It is worth reminding yourself that digression irritates the majority of readers. But there is no need to repeat it exactly. A paraphrase or the use of part of the actual title will suffice. Precise repetition, particularly if it occurs several times, suggests that you lack the ability to express the idea yourself.

2 The introduction is often at its most effective when it draws together the main points to be dealt with in the main body of the essay. It tends to have a direct quality, prepares the reader for what is to come, and helps to check the writer's natural tendency to wander from his plan. It has the further advantage of imparting a logical feel to the assignment, when the reader can see that what is promised in the introduction actually occurs in the following paragraphs. All too often, there is little connection between introduction and main body, so that, by contrast, such a start as the one suggested creates an impression of a clear and organized mind.

3 Somewhere in the introduction, you should give the reader an indication of your particular standpoint. This does not need to be too forceful or to follow the *it is my belief that/I am of the opinion that* pattern; it may be put much less personally.

4 If the above suggestions have been followed, then the introduction is likely to have provided a smooth lead into the main body, since the first main point with which one is about to deal, will already have been briefly mentioned. Should there seem to you to be a hiatus between the introduction and the main section, then there may well have been a lack of relevance, clarity or direction in the first paragraph(s). Indeed, a careful look at the junction point between sections 1 and 2 of the essay is a useful check, since you will be able to tell by the smooth or jerky transition, whether or not the introduction has done its job.

5 Avoid the temptation to list every main idea in the introduction or you may be left with nothing new to say in the conclusion. As you will note in the next section, there is a considerable tendency for the conclusion to be a barely disguised regurgitation of the introduction. Thus, it is advisable to leave one important point to be made at the end of the essay, so that it does not simply peter out.

6 It is the introduction which gives your readers their first impressions of the worth of your ideas. Too long an introduction is likely to wander from the point, to be too comprehensive, or at worst mere padding. Too short an introduction will look thin and inadequate. Ideally, the first few sentences should be a

succession of clearly expressed statements which are relevant to the title and give some indication of your personal assessment.

THE CONCLUSION

As has already been pointed out, many otherwise well-written compositions lose some credit in the very last lines, because the conclusion is almost an exact repetition of the introduction. This tendency to reproduce the opening stages of the essay in the final paragraph can be countered in a variety of ways. It may help, for instance, if you can write the end without looking back at the beginning. This is by no means foolproof, however, since ideas from the introduction are likely to resurface in the mind, when you come to concentrate on the conclusion.

If, however, you can select a specific style of closure, which is quite different from the way you led into the main body, this will avoid the danger of repetition.

STANDARD APPROACHES FOR INTRODUCTIONS AND CONCLUSIONS

(a) Agreeing or disagreeing with the title

Either at the beginning or the end of your essay, you will have to give some indication of where you stand on the issue(s) raised. As has previously been suggested, it is not necessary to make your statement into a personal credo. As the central idea in your final paragraph(s), simply state *what the author has or has not succeeded in doing/how far such-and-such a critic's objection is justified, etc*. Below are examples of what we might call *'kernel' introductory or concluding statements*:

> (i) Voltaire uses the many devices characteristic of the *conte philosophique* to produce a fast-moving tale, full of wit and irony. But *Candide* is much more than this and remains a work of universal literary, social and philosophical relevance, as much for the author's abhorrence of violence and for his commitment to suffering mankind, as for his skilful techniques.

> (ii) We have seen that the critic's objection that Ionesco's plays contain more experiment than theatre fails to take account either of the playwright's ability to build dramatic tension or of his successful use of the traditional devices of mime, farce, mobile scenery and props to maintain a lively and colourful momentum. If, at times, the action is near to gruesome pantomime, it is nonetheless theatre.

(b) Taking the middle position

You may not necessarily be in complete agreement or disagreement with the question. In such a case, it is perfectly appropriate for you to occupy the middle ground, as in the example,

> Jean Giono's novels of the Midi must in a sense be restricted by the fact that they draw so heavily on the life and characteristics of the region. They transcend this restriction in works such as *Regain*, where the author succeeds in communicating the essense of the man-woman relationship.

(c) Coming to a relative assessment

Often the question itself will not expect you to take up a polarized position, in which case your conclusion may include a drawing together of the threads along the lines of (b). Essay questions of this type look like the following:

> In what sense may Zola's *La Fortune des Rougon* be called a realist novel?
>
> How far do you find the relationship between Isaïe and Marcellin in *La Neige en deuil* to be a credible one?
>
> To what extent is Thérèse Desqueyroux a victim of her environment?

(d) Using the author (or critic)'s own statement

If you have read the background to a work you are studying sufficiently well, a quotation from it will often provide the basis for your summing-up, e.g.

> When Troyat wrote of himself that he had been 'sollicité, tour à tour, par des fantômes surannés et par des visages vrais et actuels', he might as well have been summing-up the conflict in Étienne's mind between the attractions of his dead father's monstrous past and of the goodness of the living, personified in his mother and, indeed, in Maxime Joubert.

(e) Starting with a quotation

Similarly to (d), a quotation from the author or a close contemporary may set the tone for the whole of your conclusion.

> 'Hypocrite lecteur! Mon semblable, mon frère!' Baudelaire addressed his readership in this way on more than one occasion. It is difficult to imagine the same intensity of relationship between the later Verlaine and his readers, principally because of his weak and ineffectual grip upon the life-stream. In the spuriously religious poems of *Sagesse* one so often has the impression that he is using his exceptional talent for musicality and versification as a substitute for lived experience. For Verlaine, it is as if the words come too easily.

(f) Giving a short historical background

An allusion to the background of the author or of the work will often help to set the final point that you are making.

> Given Guy de Maupassant's literary training, it is hardly surprising that one of the hallmarks of his *contes* should be their economy of style. During the period 1872–80, Maupassant was schooled by Gustave Flaubert, who insisted, almost forcibly, on a precise and unemotional use of language and of observation. The emerging writer was directed towards an objective vision and was not even allowed by Flaubert to write for publication until that aim had been achieved.

6 DRAWING UP A PLAN

Always follow a regular sequence of steps, such as:

1 Write the title at the top of your sheet.
2 Look through the margin-notes in your text-book and/or your quote-book (see pages 34–38).

3 Make a list of 6–8 brief points to form the main-body, together with page references for quotes.
4 Sketch out the Intro. Para. as a form of introductory list of these points.
5 Sketch out a Concluding Para.
6 Note any relevant external quotes or parallels in lit./films/music/radio/ theatre, etc.
7 Start writing the essay, referring whenever necessary to your plan.
8 Every time you start a new paragraph, look at your title.

7 CHECK-LIST

When you have finished writing your essay, devise a check-list such as the one below, to help you see where improvements might have been made. If the answer to several of these questions is *no*, then you should try to amend the essay, time permitting.

COMPLETED ESSAY CHECK-LIST

Have I . . . ?
  the right length?
  sufficient main-points?
  sufficient quotes?
  checked their accuracy?
  both a definite Intro. + Concln.?
  made outside reference?
  the right balance of arguments?
  looked for padding?
  looked for repetition?
  kept on theme?
  ended on a positive note?

Look through any literature essays you have written before studying this chapter. Use the check-list to help you see how you might have improved these essays.

ASSIGNMENTS

Draw up plans for the following essay topics*:

Section A (using the strong structure)
1 If you are studying a play, in which ways does it lend itself to literary study and which of its theatrical qualities are likely to escape the reader?

* Instead of producing a full plan, you may find it a useful exercise, simply to write out a list of textual references and/or quotes, which cover the points you would make.)

2 Choose one of your French authors and decide how far you agree with the statement that a knowledge of his/her background is essential to an understanding of his/her work.

3 Choose a character from one of your texts and show in which ways (s)he arouses both sympathy and irritation in the reader.

Section B (using the chronological structure)

4 Take one of your set texts and trace the development of a character of your choice.

5 Analyse the stages leading to the success or downfall of a character or strategy in a text you have studied.

6 From the reading of one of your French authors' novels/short stories/poetry, to what extent would you say his/her outlook changes throughout his/her work?

Section C (using the rolling structure)

7 What are the typical devices used by your favourite French author?

8 Analyse the main themes present in one of your texts.

9 If you have studied a French text based on historical fact, show how (in)accurate it has been in its treatment of events.

Section D (using the contrastive structure)

10 Compare and contrast two (main) characters in any work of French literature you have read.

Section E General Assignments

11 Look at the Past Paper-type essay questions on page 129 in Appendix 2 and label each one A, B, C, or D, according to which type of structure best suits it.

12 Look at pages 130–131 and list all the essays best suited to the contrastive structure.

13 For each of the French set books you have studied, produce your own list of the sort of questions you might expect at A-level. Label each one A–D, according to its type.

4

The Use of Quotations

Many people avoid direct quotation when they write a literature essay. Others pepper their essay with so many lengthy quotations that the finished product seems to be little more than extracts from the work under discussion, strung together by the odd sentence.

The answer is of course the happy medium between these two extremes. It will be an essay which is fundamentally an analysis by yourself of the work in relation to your title theme, illustrated by suitable quotations of the right length. This is fine and pious advice, but how is such a happy medium achieved? The following pointers will help you:

(a) PUNCTUATION

The selected passage should always be given between quotation marks. If it is indented from the margin, it will look neat and will stand out.

(b) THE LENGTH OF THE QUOTATION

In general, and with few exceptions, this should be 1–5 lines. In order to keep within these limits, dots may be used within the passages quoted to allow you to omit unnecessary material, as in the examples below:

> A 'Déjà, il comprenait qu'elle n'oserait jamais revenir sur leur conversation de la veille. Ayant dit ce qu'elle avait à dire, elle ne se préoccupait plus que de limiter les dégâts. À ce fils éclairé et blessé par ses soins, elle prodiguait follement les remèdes éprouvés de la tendresse et de l'habitude. Elle renouait les liens brisés, masquait les trous, chassait les ombres.'

> B 'Déjà, il comprenait qu'elle n'oserait jamais revenir sur leur conversation de la veille. Ayant dit ce qu'elle avait à dire, elle ne se préoccupait plus que de limiter les dégâts. . . . . Elle renouait les liens brisés, masquait les trous, chassait les ombres.'

> (*La Tête sur les épaules*, ch. 4)

The person producing the quotation in its condensed form is making a point about the urgent need felt by Marion to repair the quarrel with her son, Étienne. Two lines have been removed, since the rest of the material is sufficient for the point to be effective. Notice how condensation makes the point sharper.

(c) SETTING OUT THE QUOTATION

If the quote is less than a line, it may be most easily worked into a sentence in your own paragraphs, e.g.

Despite many of the unpleasant happenings in *Germinal*, Zola's outlook was fundamentally optimistic. He saw the time of justice coming for a future generation 'dont la germination allait faire bientôt éclater la terre'. Such, indeed, are the thoughts of Étienne, as he eventually leaves the mining village, which has brought so many changes to his own life.

As suggested in (a), quotations of more than one line are better separated from the paragraph containing your argument and given their own independent position on the line below, e.g.:

Man's fallibility is further underlined by the reason given by Ulysse for his decision to leave Troy in peace. Hector assumes, presumptuously, that it is his nobility of soul, only to be brought back to basic reality by the irony of Ulysse's reply:

'Pas précisément. Andromaque a le même battement de cils que Pénélope.'

Troy's fate hangs on the way Andromaque flutters her eyelashes. Little wonder that the peace is so fragile and soon to be broken irreparably.

(d) COMMENTING ON THE QUOTATION

Teachers and examiners are frequently struck by the failure of great numbers of students to make any sort of comment on the quotations they include. While the significance of certain quotes may be self-evident from the preceding essay paragraph, others, as in the previous example, will be more effective, if they are followed by a short comment, to explain them or to tie them in to the fabric of the essay.

(e) THE NUMBER OF QUOTATIONS

To a large extent this is a matter of personal choice. As a rule of thumb, the amount of material quoted should not exceed one quarter of the total length of the essay. For example, an open essay occupying four hand-written sides of A4 paper would normally be expected to contain 25–35 lines of quotation. In exam conditions you would do well to include at least 10 per cent of quotation.

(f) A QUOTE-BOOK

If you are to use your important quotations effectively, they are best kept separate from the rest of your literature notes in a quote-book, which may be kept rather like a vocabulary book. When you are studying a text either with a teacher or on your own, note down the more significant lines, keeping to the sort of maximum length already suggested, and classifying them according to characters or themes. Write in the margin the number of the text-book page on which the quotation occurs, so that you can refer back to it to refresh yourself as to the exact context, etc.

(g) LEARNING QUOTES

It is not absolutely necessary to be able to quote verbatim from a text in an examination question, but it is difficult to score high marks without doing so, since your own accuracy of recall will undoubtedly influence how clearly you remember the basic points in the argument you are putting forward.

If you have kept a quote-book, it will obviously be much easier for you to get down to the task of learning lines exactly, since you will already have an organized collection in front of you. Yet, there is still the question of how much you should learn for a particular book. It is difficult to provide a rule-of-thumb, since some people learn lines much more easily than others. However, working from the basic assumption that examinees are busy people with a great deal of other material to assimilate beside literary quotations, 40-60 lines per book should be an appropriate minimum to allow you to do well.

Of course, although this amount will often take quite a long time to learn, it will frequently represent no more than a very small fraction of the work being studied, so you will have to choose the quotations you are going to learn carefully, since they need to be representative of the book as a whole, i.e. if there are five or six types of theme likely to be encountered as exam questions, make sure you have quotations for every area.

This is not always as difficult as it sounds, since important individual quotations will often be relevant to several themes within the work. A short but good example of this is the quotation from Ulysse under (c) above. It could be used to highlight a comment on the theme of Destiny in *La Guerre de Troie n'aura pas lieu*. Similarly, it is relevant to an examination of the use of irony in the play, or of the inevitability of war, given man's fallibility, or of the character of Ulysse.

Your quote-book will be of considerable help in the tedious task of rote-learning, since, instead of having to look through the whole 60-500 pages of a text, you will find what you want arranged neatly in 5-10 pages of your own notebook, classified under clear headings.

(h) TEXT-BOOK NOTATION

This is an erudite term for what is often regarded as the cardinal sin of pencilling-in notes in the margin of your text-book. If your teacher has no objection to your marking in pencil in the margin or on the page of your book, you will find this helps you greatly to highlight the important lines on a page. The use of a system such as the one exampled below, allows you to organize a large amount of potentially quotable material in addition to that kept in your note-book, e.g.:

> *Clever style* | C'étaient quatre gros garçons à la chair blonde, à la barbe blonde, aux yeux bleus, demeurés gras malgré les fatigues qui'ils avaient endurées déjà, et bons enfants, bien qu'en pays conquis. | *starts with stereotype* ↓ *effective contrast*

Maupassant not a Germanophobe

(i) COMPILING QUOTATIONS FOR ESSAYS

One of the excellent advantages of organizing quotations along the lines suggested above, is the fact that, because you have classified small but crucial gobbets of text so clearly, you now have a system which will help you to draw up an essay-plan very quickly. Your notebook and marginal notation become a type of filing-cabinet. More often than not, you can construct a plan for a given topic simply by reference to quotable passages, as in the example:

Theme: To what extent is the atmosphere of much of 'Le Grand Meaulnes' conditioned by Seurel's basic timidity and acute uneasiness?

Page no.
14 ma mère avait constaté avec désespoir
15 je me vois épiant avec anxiété
15 j'avais regardé anxieusement du côté des cloches
16 elle s'enfermait de crainte
17 J'arrivai un peu anxieux de mon retard
19 Moi, qui n'osais plus rentrer à la maison, etc.

(j) REVISION FOR EXAMS

When exam-time looms, you are likely to be short of time. It will be unusual for you to have sufficient at your disposal to allow you to re-read all the texts before you enter the exam room.

A few hours spent looking through your marginal notes and renewing your memory of crucial questions will sometimes be enough to give you a fresh and clear picture of an individual book, if you have read it thoroughly on previous occasions. Indeed, there is a particular advantage to this approach. Since you do not have the time to re-read all of the book and are obliged to concentrate on an important digest of the material, your view of the text is often clearer, because it is not cluttered by the whole weight of the work.

Efficient exam revision is a logical and relatively painless consequence of the points discussed above, especially (f)–(i). If you have learnt a reasonable number of quotations from a book and you have kept them short, they will frequently resurface in your mind under examination conditions. You need to discipline yourself to use only those quotations which are appropriate to the theme and to use them in a correct sequence, much as you would do when compiling quotes for an essay as in (i).

(k) PRESS ARTICLES

Many examiners feel it is counterproductive for a student to produce much in the way of reference to this or that critic's view, since what is required is the student's reaction to the book, not a regurgitation or direct quotation of what eminent literati have felt about it.

However, new material referring to authors, their works and background may often appear in the Press, especially such periodicals as the (daily, *Sunday,*

Financial, and *Radio*) *Times*, the *Guardian*, *Observer* and the (Sunday) *Telegraph*. The *occasional* quotation from these sources will show initiative on your part. But you would do well to remember to avoid producing an essay full of remarks such as 'Kenneth Tyan said that . . .', 'It was Henri Peyre's belief that . . .', unless you are going to qualify their observations in some way. It is *your* views that the examiner wishes to read.

5

Reading Essay-Titles Correctly

Unfortunately, it is easy to lose yourself much credit by mis-reading essay-titles. In many cases you will not have spent enough time and care over the implications of the title. In others, an already demanding task will have been made more difficult by question compilers who seem to delight in setting complex quotations as a basis for an essay topic. Happily, literature papers are becoming far less of a maze than they used to be, since many examiners now take the view, rightly, that straightforward questions are sufficient to allow a Board to differentiate between candidates and to provide a fair assessment of their abilities.

However, you are still likely to come across at least one or two topics on your paper which will need a considerable amount of unravelling. Let us start with the most daunting type:

COMPLEX QUOTATIONS IN FRENCH

Essay titles based on quotations in French (or English) are the most difficult to treat, since, unlike a straightforward question in English, they often require you to involve yourself in a considerable amount of interpretation, before you can decide exactly what it is you are expected to comment upon. Thus, you run the very clear risk of quite literally misinterpreting the meaning of the quote and of writing an essay on a topic which may be at best unintended and at worst in no way relevant to the work under consideration.

The quotation and the accompanying question may be straightforward enough, as in:

> *How far does Sartre's famous statement 'l'enfer c'est l'autrui' sum up his attitude towards his characters in 'Huis clos'?*

However, the statement may be much more complex, as in the following example which is very similar to a question set by one of the Boards:

> *'L'absurdité, la mollesse et parfois l'obscénité du cauchemar'. Comment on this assessment of 'Les Caves du Vatican' by one of Gide's contemporaries.*

Here you have four elements to deal with: *l'absurdité/la mollesse/l'obscénité/le cauchemar*. To add to your difficulties, they are not simply isolated elements. The first three are supposed to be components of the fourth. Additionally, before you start answering the question, you will have to define *le cauchemar* in terms of Gide's novel, if you are to understand the implications of your theme.

Many teachers and examiners feel that this type of question is unfair, since it places excessive burdens on the candidate. A complex quotation runs the risk of actually encouraging the candidate to follow a false trail. Fortunately, many Boards now recognize this and there is a discernible tendency towards more straightforward questions. Even those Boards who do indulge in complex quotations still include a large number of more basic questions, the meaning of which may easily be seen, provided you have studied the work reasonably thoroughly.

If you find yourself attempting a question which is a complex quotation, there is something concrete and practical you can do, to help you isolate all the elements. It is a simple device and it will do no more than separate the individual areas to which you must give your attention. The rest will be up to you, but, at least, you will know clearly what you are supposed to be writing about.

The device is called *base and bricks*. It relies on the fact that most complex titles present several sub-themes, all contributing to the main theme, as in the Gide quotation above. If you can visualize the writing of an essay on a complex topic as the building of a small wall with a concrete base, you can represent it diagrammatically in a very simple way:

```
         ┌──────────────────┐
         │    THEME—3       │
         └──────────────────┘
         ┌──────────────────┐
         │    THEME—2       │
         └──────────────────┘
         ┌──────────────────┐
         │    THEME—1       │
         └──────────────────┘
       ┌──────────────────────┐
       │   UNIFYING POINT     │
       │     OR THEME         │
       └──────────────────────┘
```

Every time you are confronted with a complex quotation, separate it into the base and the courses above, the base being the main, unifying point. Each course of bricks is one of the principal themes contributing to it. Thus, a daunting quotation such as:

> '*Un roman à la pensée du métaphysicien et du moraliste, s'exprime dans le ton d'une satire dure jusqu'à la cruauté, indiscrète jusqu'à l'obscénité.*' Discuss this view of Sartre's '*La Nausée.*'

can be alleviated once you have established its structure:

```
              ┌──────────────┐
              │   obscenity  │
              └──────────────┘
             ┌────────────────┐
             │  indiscretion  │
             └────────────────┘
            ┌──────────────────┐
            │  cruel hardness  │
            └──────────────────┘
         ┌───────────────────────┐
         │  metaphysical novel of│
         │   observer of mankind │
         └───────────────────────┘
```

The metaphor of the wall to be built is an appropriate one. You must first work out your base, before you build your essay. Themes can be linked, as above, in the case of *obscenity* and *indiscretion*. You will, of course, add an extra level for each additional theme. If you usually have trouble organizing examples of each theme when you write an essay, you could make each brick into a specific reference to the text.

Now, look back to the Gide *cauchemar* quotation and build a wall!

'ORDINARY' ESSAY-TITLES

Having accepted that difficult or lengthy titles need close concentration, you must not forget that straightforward, brief topics need their own form of attention.

Questions such as:

Discuss the role of X in Y.
Compare and contrast the characters of A and B in C.
How far is D's attitude a reflection of E's own position?

for all their apparent simplicity, are not candidate-proof. That is, they cannot guarantee that you will produce the right material dealing with the right area of the work.

Discuss the $\boxed{\text{role}}$ *of X* can easily be interpreted as *Discuss the* $\boxed{\text{character}}$ *of X*, if you have a mind to, especially if you have not thought about what the character *does* in the work and why.

Similarly, *Compare and contrast the characters of A and B* may easily deteriorate into *Write notes on the characters of A and B*, without any effort to *compare and contrast* the qualities and behaviour of the two individuals.

Some examination candidates actually go as far as completely ignoring one character or the other, either through lack of textual knowledge, or because they find one easier to write on than the other. It is impossible for them to obtain a pass-mark for such an answer.

Undoubtedly, there is often a tendency, especially in exam conditions, for some candidates to succumb to what one might term a *latch-on* effect. That is, for reasons of over- or of under-confidence, they skim through a title and *latch on* to a few words, which they construe as they want. Thus, the third example question above becomes:

Give a summary of D's attitude

which, once more, is not at all what is being asked.

Whenever you have to choose a literary essay topic, look closely at key-words like:

role/contrast/compare/significance/analyse/assess/function/purpose

and treat them with proper respect.

AGREEING WITH THE QUESTION

Naturally, when you have gone to the trouble of studying and entering for an exam, you want to pass it. Because of this simple fact, you may suffer from a very understandable tendency to try to ingratiate yourself with your examiners or teachers by agreeing with everything in the essay-title in front of you. This is especially true in *How far* ...? questions:

> How far does Anatole France succeed in producing credible female characters in *'Les Dieux ont soif'*?
> How far do you agree with the judgement that in *L'Enfant*, Vallès 'dishonours the family, especially the mother'?
> What truth is there in the statement that Musset's poetry is irrelevant to the late twentieth-century reader?

The key to your reaction actually lies in the *qualified* nature of the questions *How far* ...? and *What truth* ...? With any or all three of the sample questions, you might be expected to be in *qualified* agreement with the underlying point. But this means that there will be some divergences. There will be some implications of the work for which the comment is not valid and you should try to provide a balanced assessment. You should show where the judgement is correct and where it is not so.

Always be on the look-out for questions where you do not have to be in total agreement with the main point of the title.

6

Character Analysis

Both during your A-level course and in the actual examination, you will be presented with essay questions relating to individual characters, their development, their function or role within a work, the author's attitude to them, and their inter-relationship with other characters or elements.

In most novels, short stories and plays, and in some poetry, the characters and the way they behave and grow will be central to an understanding of the work and of the author's purpose. Why is this?

In some ways, a prose work is like a photograph album. Imagine an album filled with photographs of land-, sea- and town-scapes, where the photographer has decided to take a group of pictures containing no interesting people. Most of us would react to the album in a fairly predictable manner. Yes, a pleasant series of pretty pictures, but they are somehow incomplete. It is the people and animals who inhabit these places who give them much of their meaning, since our life is a combination of the places in which we find ourselves and the people with whom we have contact.

Thus, a successful writer must have some ability to produce characters and to flesh them out, so that they come alive and interact in a way that contributes something to the central purpose of the work.

Your task is to assess just how successful the author has been in producing characters who are credible and who fulfil the role for which they were intended.

To do this, you need to analyse your own reactions, as well as those of the personality under your microscope. This means you will often have to walk something of a tight-rope. It may be good for you to react strongly to fictional people, but it will not be good if your emotions are so strong that you lose the ability to treat them rationally.

For example, you may find a character to be petty, soulless, aggressive and conceited. Your next step is not to feel particularly hostile to him every time he crops up in the work, but, rather, to ask yourself the following questions:

   (a) Am I meant to see this person as such an unpleasant individual, or am I reading into the text things which are not there?
   (b) If I am intended to react as I have done, what is the author's purpose?

THE AUTHOR'S PURPOSE

The character will not have arrived in the work by accident. In the real world, all types of people will move in and out of our lives randomly, but, because a novel or a play is a fictionalized and nearly always concertina-ed slice of life, virtually all its people will have been included to some purpose. A writer simply cannot afford the space to allow a variety of incidental characters to stroll through the pages of the work. Therefore any person who appears more than fleetingly has to earn his or her keep.

This state of affairs will actually help you in writing essays, since you can be sure that almost all characters will have some significance. Your first task may be to determine just what this significance is. Most important characters are likely to fulfil one or more of the following roles, as:

THE AUTHOR'S MAIN CONCERN

A person under emotional, psychological or environmental stress/a maturing or deteriorating individual/a mirror of the age or of social conditions/an object lesson.

A CATALYST

A device to help the action along or to precipitate a situation. In Ionesco's *Le roi se meurt*, for example, the young queen, Marie, could be referred to as a catalyst, since her behaviour and persona force the old queen into action to save Bérenger from the worst excesses of his own nature.

Sometimes the function of an individual in a story will be particularly obvious, but before you make any attempt to determine his role, it will pay dividends to look at his character. Clearly, if you know well what sort of a person you are dealing with, you will be in a better position to say exactly why that person has a place in the work.

PERSONALITY

It is not always as easy to assess the personality of a character in fiction as it is that of someone you know in real life. The reason for this is very basic. A book gives you less to go on than months or years of frequent exposure to a real person. So, in a book you will have to look more carefully and make good use of the smaller amounts of information given to you.

However, you *will* have the advantage that the author will often state quite categorically several of a person's traits. Nevertheles, deciding what someone's character is like is not particularly easy, even in the real situation.

Most people tend to make value-judgements about people on a snap basis; for instance, if they have been especially sly or helpful towards us on one or two occasions, then they are assumed to be generally cunning or amiable. For the most part, you will tend to categorize people as nice or not nice, friendly or unfriendly, without going into every single reason why. Yet, when you analyse a character in a book, you are expected to produce an accurate and balanced assessment.

INDIVIDUAL TRAITS AND A CHARACTER-PROFILE

Picking over the bones of a fictional person's character, then, is not easy, but it should not prove impossible. Look at the character-profile on page 46 and you will see a long list of individual qualities. Before trying to pick out specific traits belonging to a figure in one of your set-texts, you will find it helpful to assess the broad basis of the persona.

Instead of starting, for example, by wondering whether (s)he is sympathetic/conceited/tragic/neurotic, etc., ask yourself:

Is this person generally a positive or a negative individual?
Is there a side of his/her character which clashes with the general picture he/she presents?
Is my reaction to him/her sympathetic or not?
What are his/her two or three most striking characteristics?

If you follow this procedure, your analysis will probably develop along the following lines:

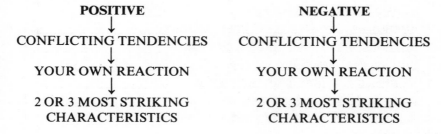

POSITIVE	NEGATIVE
↓	↓
CONFLICTING TENDENCIES	CONFLICTING TENDENCIES
↓	↓
YOUR OWN REACTION	YOUR OWN REACTION
↓	↓
2 OR 3 MOST STRIKING CHARACTERISTICS	2 OR 3 MOST STRIKING CHARACTERISTICS

ASSIGNMENT

The character-profile is explained in detail below. Before using it for literary character-analysis, choose four people whom you know well at home or in school and try to select from the list in the profile *ten* personality traits, which you think fit each of these real people. It may be advisable not to make the results too public, as most people do not like being reminded of their foibles!

CHARACTER PROFILE

From each row, select one or two* adjectives which describe the character under consideration and write them in the box at the side. Score the items in the box on the scale 1–3, e.g.

sympathetic–3; impulsive–1;

indicates the individual is very sympathetic and a little impulsive.

Title of Work: . . . .   *Character:* . . . .

PROFILE-BOX

Adjectives	
sympathetic conceited tragic neurotic	
distant impulsive wise cowardly	
weak overbearing carefree resentful	
strong comic anxious generous	
irrational humanitarian brave prudent	
proud violent considerate warm	
relaxed mournful magnanimous sinister	
compassionate ruthless progressive feckless	
aggressive affectionate conservative calm	
wary modest demanding scornful	
world-weary scolding coarse exuberant	
gentle hopeless humorous energetic	
despairing cheerful humble morbid	
happy hopeful passive insecure	
passionate petty forgiving confident	
serious pessimistic sad refined	
soulless boorish earthy determined	

other qualities not listed: . . . .

Notes to be read before completing the profile:

* Unless it is absolutely necessary do NOT select more than at most two qualities from any one line.

Do not feel obliged to fill in each line of the box. It is likely that there will be some lines in which none of the qualities fits the character you are examining.

When you have completed the box, find examples in your text which illustrate each point of character.

N.B. IF a character in the work under study changes considerably during the course of events, complete a profile for him/her as he/she appears on both early and later acquaintance.

USING THE CHARACTER-PROFILE

Each line of the profile contains four qualities or attitudes. Normally, you would not expect to find more than two from a line in any one individual. When you are required to analyse a literary character, work your way through the grid line by line. With each line, decide which (if any) of the traits is/are discernible in the character under examination, write the trait(s) in the profile-box and try to give page references to passages in the text illustrating the point.

When you have completed the profile-box, you are likely to have uncovered a reasonably large number of traits. Now decide which of these are most significant in the character's make-up and in his/her role in the work. Concentrate on these in your essay and bring in the points of lesser significance only if they should prove relevant.

ASSIGNMENT

Take *three* important characters from the French texts you have studied so far and use the profile to help you to draw up a list of their traits. For each character, sum up in 4–5 lines your personal reaction, in as unemotional terms as possible.

CHARACTER DEVELOPMENT

Your task in assessing character is not always simply a question of producing a list of an individual's strengths and weaknesses. Often, a character will show a steady development or major change during the course of the work you are studying. Part of your brief is to note the stages in this change.

Always ask yourself the question, *Are this person's behaviour and attitudes really static or has there been some noticeable change?*

The central point or interest of the work may in fact hinge upon such a change, as in *La Tête sur les épaules*, where Étienne is forced by the coincidence of external events and pressures to grow up quickly enough to be able to accept his responsibilities as a young adult.

One of the major themes in Colette's *Le Blé en herbe* is the change in two adolescents over the years. But not all developments in character and changes in attitudes and reactions are so evident as in these two works about young people reaching adulthood.

In such a large work as Zola's *Germinal*, for example, many things happen to Étienne and the changes wrought in him are more gradual and take longer to occur. At the end of the novel, Étienne has undoubtedly been modified and sometimes chastened by his experiences, but he moves on to new pastures, maintaining the optimism with which he arrived at the mining village of Montsou:

À gauche, à droite, plus loin, il croyait en reconnaître d'autres sous les blés, les haies vives, les jeunes arbres. Maintenant, en plein ciel, le ciel d'avril rayonnait dans sa gloire, échauffant la terre qui enfantait.

From this passage, we gain an impression of the epic nature of the stage on which Étienne's life is being played out and, when, again in the last pages, Zola says of his young hero that *sa raison mûrissait*, we realize most clearly that the elements of his character and the development of his personality are inter-linked.

It is this linkage, you will find, in many an essay on character, that you must try to define by describing both the various facets of the person's make-up and the way (s)he develops during the course of the work.

ASSIGNMENTS

1 Choose a main character from one of your set-books and, using short quotations, show how his/her character develops or remains static during the course of the work.

2 Select 4–6 example passages in a book you are studying to illustrate any *one* of the following qualities in a character of your choice:

   sympathetic/distant/weak/overbearing/comic/tragic/violent/irrational/impulsive/proud/wise/humanitarian/kind/inadequate/anxious/carefree/evil

3 Look back at the list of qualities in the last Assignment and name for each one any character you have encountered who fits the description.

4 Think of an unpleasant character in a set-book. Try to locate instances in the text, which show him/her to have redeeming characteristics.

5 Is there any character you have encountered in French literature whose behaviour sometimes seems markedly inconsistent with his/her normal actions? Find example passages in the text to prove your point.

6 Find a character to whom you relate very positively. Give short examples from the text to show why you like him/her.

7 Do the same for a character whom you dislike.

8 Choose a character from a set-book, who reminds you of someone you have seen in a film. Make notes on their similarities.

9 Think of a character in real life who resembles one of the characters in a French book you have read. Make notes on their similarities.

10 Can you find a character in a set-book who is simply not true to life? Give 4–6 short examples of his/her behaviour to prove your point.

11 Study the behaviour of a character in a set-book and describe where it is typically French.

12 Do you know a work in which any main character resembles the author? Find 3–4 sample passages to support your view.

13 If any main character resembles a famous historical person, find passages in the work which illustrate this similarity.

14 Find 4–6 example passages in which one of your authors uses physical description to convey character.

15 Is there a conflict between the characters of two of the main protagonists in any of the French books that you have read? If so, find 3–5 points of contrast between the two people.

16 Is there a character in any of your set-books who is essentially tragic? Draw examples from the text to show exactly what it is which makes the individual tragic.

7

The Novel or Short-story Essay

In some respects it is easier to write an essay about a novel, or a collection of short stories, than to deal with some of the more specialized aspects of drama or of poetry. However, prose narratives have their own technicalities, which you should always bear in mind. Most of these technical points are concerned with the structure of the prose work.

If you learn to look for the elements and devices used by authors in building their finished works, this will help you, not simply to write an essay on, say, the structure of a novel, but, more often, to include general points on composition in essays relating to wider themes. In other words, the structure of the work will almost always be significant in questions on say character, plot, social themes, since the way the book is built up goes a long way towards determining how you react to an individual within the story, or to the concluson of the tale, and so on.

For example, if an author spends a great deal of time building up detail in a painstaking manner, rather in the way that life itself often evolves slowly, then you are likely to see characters within the work as fully-drawn individuals. If another author concentrates on the description of the natural background and spends proportionately less time on the characters, then you will either see the people in the story very much as creations of their environment, or you will gain the impression that the author is less concerned with human beings than with the (natural) world which surrounds them.

Questions on basic structure tend to look like the following:

(a) What elements does ... use to create a picture of sophisticated life in ... ?

(b) In what ways can ... be said to be a romantic/naturalistic/surrealist novel?

(c) How far can ... be said to be the work of an experimentalist?

(d) Which devices does ... use to maintain the reader's interest throughout the work?

(e) How does ... maintain the tension/action/story-line throughout the work?

(f) How far does ... succeed in his/her basic purpose in writing ... ?

However, other examination questions may focus on structure within a work, as in

(g) What use does the author make of an episodic technique in ... ?

(h) Why is background so important in ... ?

(i) What use does the author make of the ... motif in ... ?

(j) What part does silence play in ... ?

(k) What does the author achieve through his use of a cinema flash-back technique in ...?

(l) Where in ... does the author depart from his theoretical naturalism?

(m) How successful is the author in the innovations she uses in ...?

ASSIGNMENTS

1 Take any of the question-types (a)–(f) above, adapt it to one of your set-books and draw up an essay-plan, concentrating on the points of structure discussed below.

2 Follow the same procedure with any one question-type from (g) to (m). Remember that you may well have to adapt, so that your title may become something like *Why is the FAMILY so important in ...?* or *What part does MUSIC play in ...?*, etc.

So that you may be able to analyse the building-blocks of a work of prose narrative, let us look at the basic elements of structure in some detail.

1 THE BASIC NARRATIVE TECHNIQUE

This is the foundation on which the rest of the work will be built. Ask yourself these questions:

Is the narrative smooth-flowing or does the author deliberately hold it up at times?

Does it follow a straightforward chronological sequence or does it adopt an episodic pattern in which the chapters or sections are distinct and deliberately separate?

At the beginning of a new section, does the author go back somewhat in time, to look at a different character's involvement in the action?

Is the narrative divided into neat chapters/sections, or is it one continuous flow?

Do the episodes follow each other in a logical sequence, or does the author keep switching backwards and forwards in time?

What is the purpose of the basic technique?

Is it to involve/distance the reader?

Does it underline the complex relationships between individual lives and events?

Is one made to feel that characters are leading largely separated and isolated/inter-connected lives?

Does the author allow his/her personal attitudes to intrude?

If so, is this achieved by frequent interventions/occasional very direct comments/the placing side-by-side of contrasting situations and events/historical allusions/the use of parables/the inclusion of a great deal of emotive imagery and events?

Does the author take us into his/her confidence or are we kept in suspense? For what reasons?

Is the detail carefully worked out or are there clear flaws in the compilation of the narrative?

Why does the author pay so much attention to detail/appear to disregard the need for accuracy?

BACKGROUND

In most cases the backcloth against which the characters play out their roles will have a major effect on the way they are seen. If the author does no more than give a few brief touches of background, then the reader will be obliged to concentrate on the action in which the characters are involved.

At this point, perhaps we should clarify the meaning of the term *background*. The word has wider implications than the past life and circumstances of the person being studied. *Backcloth* may be a helpful word here, since *background* really means the whole of the environment, past and present, surrounding a character.

What are the implications of such a background for the individuals under the literary microscope? What effect has the individual's town/city/country/sea/foreign/sheltered/lively/crude/sophisticated environment provoked? Is the character a product of that environment? Does (s)he accept it or rebel against it? Is it a background which is accurately portrayed and readily recognized or is it highly artificial?

ASSIGNMENT

3 Analyse the background in any of your set texts and make a list of those elements which have not been listed in the preceding paragraph.

3 THE USE OF MOTIFS

Often, a novel or series of short stories will contain a motif, a recurring device which may symbolize an aspect of one of the characters, the author's own attitude to the work, etc. In Zola's *Germinal*, for example, the mine itself becomes a central character, and is frequently described as an animal, monstrous and insatiable:

C'était fini, la bête mauvaise, accroupie dans ce creux, gorgée de chair humaine, ne soufflait plus de son haleine grosse et longue.

Flaubert employs the image of a carthorse to render Charles Bovary's plodding manner and lack of imagination in *Madame Bovary* –

Il accomplissait sa petite tâche quotidienne à la manière du cheval de manège, qui tourne en place les yeux bandés, ignorant de la besogne qu'il broie.

This is a most telling motif, since the picture of a blinkered working horse, awkward and lacking in self-awareness, makes it difficult if not impossible for the reader to take Charles seriously on several levels.

ASSIGNMENT

4 Look for a recurring motif in any of your French set books and make a list of
the occasions on which it occurs in the text.

4 THE USE OF DIALOGUE

Somehow, the importance of dialogue in a prose work tends to be glossed over.
It is almost as if the narrative were the only important thing and the passages of
speech were included merely to fill a few gaps. Yet, dialogue is a vital element,
since it reveals so much about characters and the way they interact. It may be
used:

(a) TO GIVE PACE AND VARIETY TO THE TEXT

Basic narrative requires more concentration from the reader than is normally
the case with speech. Passages of conversation will often break up the pattern
and give the work a lighter touch. If you look at the dialogue in one of your
texts, provided it is done well, you will see how people do not talk in paragraphs
and in chunks of ten lines or so. Many utterances may be just a few words and
they can be highly colloquial without detracting from the author's good style.

In a psychological novel like *La Tête sur les épaules*, Troyat will use such
conversation, not simply to give his readers some relief, but also to show the
more normal side of the environment of a late adolescent in crisis:

> – *Nous nous reverrons, chuchota-t-elle.*
> – *Si vous voulez.*
> *Un peu de joie se mêla à son amertume.*
>   *Oui, je le veux, dit-elle avec une effronterie subite. Vous m'intéressez beaucoup.*
> – *Pourquoi?*
> – *Parce que vous êtes un drôle de coco.*

This is a moment of contact between two young people which all of us will
recognize. It has vitality and brings us to the next function of dialogue.

(b) TO PROVIDE REALISM

The above extract does more than add a little pace and variety to a tale. It has
a whiff of realism about it, which is frequently much more difficult to convey in
the narrative prose. There is good reason why this should be so. Not all of us
read books, but talk is something we all indulge in, frequently. We are, therefore,
very familiar with the nuances of speech. What people say in a novel or short
story, provided the author knows what he is about, will have a direct appeal to
us. When Yolande, who has met Étienne only that evening, calls him a *queer fish*
in the conversation above, we identify immediately with what she says, even if
we personally might have put it in a slightly different way.

Note also the snappiness of the dialogue, the irony, the conflicting emotions, the picture presented to others by Étienne. There is a reality here, which it is very difficult for simple narrative to obtain.

(c) TO CONVEY CONFLICT AND TO PROVIDE DRAMATIC TENSION

Dialogue is essentially a catechism, a process of questioning and answering, involving two or more people. It is consequently an ideal means of conveying conflict, be it large or small. Let us stay with *La Tête sur les épaules* for a moment and note how Troyat uses conversation to bring out some of the essentials of the mother-son relationship existing between Marion and Étienne:

> – À la place de M. Maxime Joubert, je te retiendrais pour dîner, dit Étienne.
> Elle éclata de rire en secouant ses cheveux courts:
> – M. Maxime Joubert a bien d'autres soucis en tête. Nous nous voyons pour parler affaires. . . .
> – Et il t'envoie des fleurs!
> – Parce que c'est un galant homme.
> – Parce qu'il te trouve à son goût.
> – Tu es stupide, Étienne! Je te défends . . .

You will have noted for yourself the strength of feeling with which Étienne refers to Maxime Joubert. His jealousy is self-evident and strikes immediate chords for the reader. We have all been jealous at some time or other and most of us have used words like these, or wanted to use them. Conversation reaches right to us.

There are other reasons for using dialogue, such as the need to show the contrast between a character's thoughts and his or her actions, but the three above categories will provide the major justification. Whenever possible, look at the function of conversation in the work you are studying and refer to it in an essay on structure, style, character, themes, etc. It will almost always be relevant to an essay topic.

ASSIGNMENTS

5 Find six examples in any one of your French texts where the author uses dialogue to give pace and variety.
6 Find as many examples as you can in any one of your set-books of the author's use of dialogue to provide realism.
7 Look through all your French texts and find two or three examples in each, where dialogue has been employed as a means of conveying conflict.

5 INNOVATION AND EXPERIMENT

One of the more significant aspects of the structure of the work may be the author's use of new techniques, or the borrowing of strategies from other media.

The cinema has proved a source of inspiration for many writers, such as Troyat in *La Neige en deuil*, who have used its flashback technique to record vivid impressions. At crucial points in the narrative, the reader will be shot back with the character to an event in the past, before being returned to the present narrative.

The spectacular success of the thriller, both in the cinema and as a popular form of fiction, has had a considerable success on serious writers. When you are studying the structure of a novel, look for loose ends which are not picked up till later in the action and for a preponderance of chapters which end on a note of suspense.

A development running contemporaneously with the modern cinema has been the *new novel*, including the work of authors such as Butor and Alain Robbe-Grillet, which is deliberately ambiguous and inconsistent. It may also take the form of a continuous piece of prose in which little seems to happen.

In a sense, there have always been new novelists, just as there have been new artists. Writers have come to prominence with the arrival of new theories and schools in literature. When Naturalism arose in the second half of the nineteenth century, Zola, in particular, adapted the novel to the tenets of this socio-political movement. If you are studying Zola, look at your text to see how Zola's beliefs have conditioned the structure. How does he develop the theme of a person's life determined by heredity and circumstances? What does he do to the plot and his characters to make a thinly-disguised political appeal to his readership?

If Zola is not one of your set authors, but you have another who is identified with a movement, such as Sartre with Existentialism or Breton with Surrealism, look to see how the writer's beliefs have conditioned the structure of the work. To help yourself, ask the question: *How is this work different from what is being written today?* Ask yourself also if there is some evidence of obsession in the work.

The world of music has also influenced certain novelists. If you are studying Gide's *Symphonie pastorale*, look for its effect on the structure of that work. Marguerite Duras' exceptional novel *Moderato Cantabile* has a structure which is in a sense almost totally musical. If you are studying this text, analyse its sections.

ASSIGNMENTS

8 Find any evidence you can of the use of cinema techniques in any of your set texts.

9 Is any of your authors a *method writer*, i.e. someone writing to a set formula and sticking very closely to the tenets of a particular movement? Find six examples from the text to prove the point.

10 Someone who is wholly a method writer is hardly likely to be a great author. If you have answered 9, find six specific examples in the work, where the author escapes the limitations of the structure to good purpose.

11 If you are studying an author who uses music or a diary format to structure his/her work, list 6–8 suitable passages from the text, to show how this is done.

8

The Drama Essay

In some ways it is unfortunate that you should have to write literature essays about drama, since plays are meant to be acted, heard and seen, rather than simply read.

The reason that so many plays are studied as literature is that the language they contain has sufficient meaning and depth to it for the work to be studied as a book. Yet it should never be forgotten that the prime quality in any play is its action, or, at least, the activity that occurs between certain of the characters.

When you actually *see* a play in the theatre, what strikes you most are the colour, movement and dramatic tension. You should not leave these out of consideration when you come to write about a play.

Of course, your basic task may often be to analyse the development of an individual's personality within the work, or the relationship between the characters, or a variety of other factors related to themes such as historical accuracy, the author's purpose, his use of source materials, etc. You will inevitably concentrate on an analysis using the type of method developed on pages 22–23, but if you do not try to *see* the play in your mind's eye, as if you had actually been in the audience, you will not be doing justice to the work. The author, who is not just an author, but a playwright, has to develop the whole of the play, not just the written lines.

A useful, though not complete, analogy would be a comparison with the composer who produces an attractive song. The melody-line is undoubtedly vital to its success, but without a base and various items of orchestration, the tune may never reach its full potential.

Let us look at Molière's famous play *Le Tartuffe* as a clear example of the need to bear the theatrical aspects of the work in mind. As with most of Molière's theatre, the play was written partly to instruct and partly to entertain. There is a well-known scene within *Le Tartuffe*, in which Mme Elvire attempts to prove to her husband that the title-character is a posturing, religious bigot, who has designs upon her honour. A trap is set for Tartuffe, for whom an interview with Elvire in private is arranged. Her husband, however, is secreted into the room and hidden under a table.

Here is the basis for a scene with considerable comic possibilities. The lines spoken by the characters are witty, sharp and entertaining, as you would expect of Molière. Anyone reading the play would profit from it. But the effect and the significance of the confrontation would be greatly increased if (s)he were aware of the fact that Molière stipulated a specific stage-direction whereby the table concealing the outraged husband has one side open to the audience, so that they may *see* how he reacts, while the designing Tartuffe is oblivious to his presence. Thus, an important element of this scene is its visual impact and, if the reader is unaware of it, then his or her understanding and enjoyment is incomplete.

THE THEATRICAL ELEMENTS

When you read a play, what are the especially theatrical elements to keep in mind as possible contributors to the picture you are attempting to piece together?

You should look principally at the stage directions, movement, music, dramatic tension, audience involvement, colour, and use of dialect within the work.

THE STAGE DIRECTIONS

This is the easiest 'orchestrative' element for the reader to locate, since it is always given in the text in black and white. Before you write a drama essay, always look to find out whether the stage directions make a significant contribution to the play in general and to the theme you are analysing in particular.

By way of example, look at the following extract from Ionesco's *Le Roi se meurt** and see if you can decide in what way the stage directions contribute to the effectiveness of the action:

Tournant autour du Roi, Marguerite coupe dans le vide, comme si elle avait dans les mains des ciseaux invisibles.

Le Roi: Moi. Moi. Moi.

Marguerite: Ce n'est pas toi. Ce sont des objets étrangers, des adhérences, des parasites monstrueux. Le gui poussant sur la branche, le lierre qui grimpe sur le mur n'est pas le mur. Tu ploies sous le fardeau, tes épaules sont courbées, c'est cela qui te vieillit. Et ces boulets que tu traînes, c'est cela qui entrave ta marche.

(*Marguerite se penche, elle enlève des boulets invisibles des pieds du Roi, puis elle se relève en ayant l'air de faire un grand effort pour soulever les boulets.*) Des tonnes, des tonnes, ça pèse des tonnes.

(*Elle fait mine de jeter ces boulets en direction de la salle puis se redresse allégée.*) Ouf! Comment as-tu pu traîner cela toute une vie! (*Le Roi essaye de se redresser.*) Je me demandais pourquoi tu étais voûté, c'est à cause de ce sac. (*Marguerite fait mine d'enlever un sac des épaules du Roi et de le jeter.*) Et de cette besace. (*Même geste de Marguerite pour la besace.*) Et de ces godasses de rechange.

Le Roi, sorte de grognement. Non.

Marguerite. Du calme! Tu n'en auras plus besoin de ces chaussures de rechange. Ni de cette carabine, ni de cette mitraillette. (*Même gestes que pour la besace.*) Ni de cette boîte à outils. (*Mêmes gestes; protestation du Roi.*) Ni de ce sabre. Il a l'air d'y tenir. Un vieux sabre, tout rouillé. (*Elle le lui enlève bien que le Roi s'y oppose maladroitement.*) Laisse-moi donc faire. Sois sage.

* For a full commentary on this passage, see the example context-question answer on pages 81–83.

It is impossible to assess the real significance of a work like *Le Roi se meurt* without taking the stage directions into account. They help us to envisage the physical action which is occurring, but, equally important, they complement the significance of the spoken lines, since what is said is linked inextricably with the physical action on stage.

Let us examine the specific significance of some of the directions.

Tournant autour du Roi ...
Mime has a vital role in the plays of Ionesco. Two of its more basic functions are: (1) to underline the ludicrous, the incongruous and the pathetic in much of what we do; (2) to impart a *symbolical* nature to some of the characters' actions. Here, Marguerite, by her mimed actions, underlines in a symbolical manner the fact that the King, Béranger, is cutting his links with his life, or, rather, is being helped into cutting them.

Marguerite se penche ...
These directions, when followed, continue to convey to the audience a visual allegory of the King's journey into death and also of the great efforts made by Marguérite to help him along his lonely road.

There is an immediacy about mime, since the lack of a spoken message obliges the audience to concentrate more firmly on the evidence of their eyes. Consequently, it is particularly effective for establishing (a) the poignancy of the character's position (b) involving the audience and creating an emotional response. Anybody who has seen the work of the great French mime, Marcel Marceau, will have experienced this involvement.

Elle fait mine ...
Continues the effect.

se redresse allégée ...
brings the audience temporary relief from the tension.

Le Roi essaye de se redresser
Gives the reader an impression of what the audience will have seen, namely, the infirmity of the King, whose incapacity increases all the while.

Marguerite fait mine ...
It is important to note from the directions, how often Marguerite comes to the King's aid. *C'est à cause de ce sac. Et de cette besace* has less significance for readers who do not use the evidence of the directions to see how strongly Marguerite is working for Bérenger.

Sorte de grognement
There is pathos here, besides more evidence of the contrast between Béranger's ever-increasing feebleness and the strength, resolve and commitment of the Queen Marguerite.

MOVEMENT OR PACE

In order to keep the audience involved in the play, a good playwright will vary the movement or the pace of the action. When you are studying a play, always look to see what pace it has. There are several devices used to give a feeling of movement.

The first of these is the use of short scenes to balance the effect of longer ones. Molière is particularly adept at the production of such scenes and will often create them, to bring home to the audience the basic point he is making, as in *Le Tartuffe*, Act V, Scene 5

> *Orgon:* Hé bien, vous le voyez, ma mère, si j'ai droit,
> Et vous pouvez juger du reste par l'exploit:
> Ses trahisons enfin vous sont-elles connues?
> *Madame Pernelle:* Je suis tout ébaubie, et je tombe des nues!

Such scenes create a rapidity of movement, which tends to carry along the audience with it.

In plays with relatively few scenes changes, a feeling of pace will have to be produced through exchanges involving a great deal of short statement and counter-statement, or by the characters involving themselves in a whole series of minor actions to break up the dialogue. If you were studying Anouilh's *Becket*, then a comment on the pace of the dialogue between the four barons at the beginning of Act 2 would be appropriate to many essays:

> *1er Baron:* Je peux donc me poser la question.
> *2e Baron;* Quelle question?
> *1er Baron:* De savoir qui c'est ce Becket.
> *2e Baron:* Comment qui c'est ce Becket? C'est le chancelier d'Angleterre.
> *1er Baron:* Oui, mais je me pose la question de savoir, en tant qu'homme, ce qu'il est.
> *2e Baron:* (*le regarde et conclut, triste*) Tu as mal quelque part?
> *1er Baron:* Pourquoi?
> *2e Baron:* Parce qu'un baron qui se pose des questions est un baron malade.

Even taken out of context, the conversation has the flavour of the music hall.

In *La dernière Bande*, a very short play with one character, Samuel Beckett employs several series of minor actions to break up the monologue

Krapp débranche l'appareil, rêvasse. Finalement il farfouille dans ses poches, rencontre la banane, la sort, l'examine de tout près, la remet, farfouille de nouveau, remet l'enveloppe, regarde sa montre, se lève et s'en va au fond de la scène dans l'obscurité.

Comment on the pace of the play will be relevant to most of the essays that you will be required to write.

MUSIC

It is easy to ignore the stage directions when reading a play, especially that part concerning the music to be employed. This is because it is hard to imagine the music, when in your class-reading and in your essay-preparation, you are concentrating on the thought and the words of which the play is built up. Yet, a little imagination can help you to realize how much the music may add to the scene and to the play as a whole.

For instance, in the stage directions relating to the décor at the beginning of *Le Roi se meurt*, we read:

> *Avant le lever du rideau, pendant que le rideau se lève et quelques instants encore, on entend une musique dérisoirement royale, imitée d'après les Levers du Roi du XVIIe siècle.*

It is the *dérisoirement royale* which communicates in musical tones much of the feel of an incongruous world, so prevalent in the early stages of the play.

In what concrete ways can a reference to the music be made, other than in an essay on the structure of the work?

In an essay on Bérenger's character, you could make the point that the music acts almost as a signature-tune, for a king whose own fitness to rule is now much in question. The music imparts most strongly the impression of a king at odds with himself and with his world.

For an essay on the various techniques employed by Ionesco in his stagecraft, you would be able to mention the use of music as a sound equivalent of many of the visual impressions of a crumbling world.

Look for any use of music in the play you are studying and ask yourself the crucial question:

> *How does the music enhance the total effect of the work?*

COLOUR

Unfortunately, when you read a play you are in a worse position than someone with a black and white television set who yearns for colour. At least this person has the advantage of being able to see the characters and the scene, to watch the movement and to hear the words, sound effects and music as they are actually produced.

You, with only the printed text in front of you, will often have no more than the stage directions to guide you. So, again, try to let your imagination take over. Find out what you can from the text as to what costumes are being worn, how rich the sets are, how much furniture and bric-a-brac are to be used. In a strange sort of way, this will help you to peg-down the sometimes disembodied voices which come to you from the lines on the page.

Often the use of colour, or the partial suppression of it, may be crucial to the playwright's purpose. It is most important, for instance, to know why Genet makes so much use of colourful, flamboyant and highly bizarre costume in his plays. Similarly, Anouilh's insistence on a classical simplicity of dress, with modest backcloths and few props in *Antigone* is of considerable significance.

Always ask the question:

What use does the author make of colour in the play?

DRAMATIC TENSION

This is an element which will require less delving on your part. If the play is read effectively in class, much of the tension will come out. Nonetheless, you will be even more aware of its presence, if you make a specific search for the devices which produce it. Look for:

1 clashes of personality or character
2 the mixing of long and short scenes
3 scenes containing a preponderance of short lines or speeches
4 a plot with many twists and turns
5 a *deus ex machina* (= a surprise intervention)
6 scenes ending on a high point
7 the frequent introduction of innuendo
8 misfortune befalling a sympathetic character
9 a race against time
10 protagonists acting in ignorance of a situation of which the audience have prior knowledge
11 strong emotional appeals to the audience
12 the introduction of characters symbolizing good and evil
13 gripping physical action
14 audience involvement

   Many of the observations you make in relation to the dramatic tension of a play will also be relevant in essays on character, style, the author's position, the general worth of the work.

AUDIENCE INVOLVEMENT

This is a feature of many plays of which you may not be aware, unless you have been to the theatre quite often. Again, the stage directions may be of help to you, but, often, a producer will take the decision for him or herself to involve patrons in certain parts of the play.
   This may be nothing more than the colourful pantomime technique of having everybody join in a song with some of the characters. On the other hand, a character being chased may run into the audience, passing through the rows and along the steps, as (s)he goes.
   Alternatively, one of the principals may address specific individuals in the audience from the boards and may even go as far as expecting an answer from them. He or she may occasionally leave the boards and talk with the people in the auditorium. (S)he may ridicule them or appeal to their sense of reason.
   When you are reading a play in class, look for the possibilities for such audience involvement.

DIALECT

When reading the text of the play, it is easy to ignore the most obvious speech-related device which the author will use. Somehow, we have long fallen into the trap of believing that *proper* plays are spoken in *proper* accents, otherwise known as *received pronunciation* or *standard English.*

This process of *standardization* used to be common to both the English and French theatres, but the last twenty years have seen a movement back towards the use of normal, natural accents in plays, as the playwrights intended them to sound.

Such a principle is important and not merely a whim, since accent, used effectively, can have a decisive effect on the impact of a character in a scene and throughout a whole play. A case in point is the Guard in *Antigone*, whose robust Black Country, Geordie or Welsh accent contrasts strikingly with the measured tones of the principal protagonists, Antigone and her uncle, Creon. Every time he speaks, he brings vibrancy and a sense of relief into a highly charged debate centring on Antigone's wish to do away with herself. At times he is comic, he is almost always rough, but his very ordinariness and the vigour of his speech draw off the tension when it is becoming too much for the audience.

The present author has seen performances of the play in which the following lines have been spoken in tones more appropriate to a newscaster than to a rough diamond. One can easily imagine the effect, or the lack of it:

> *J'ai dix-sept ans de service. Je suis engagé volontaire, la médaille, deux citations. Je suis bien noté, chef. Moi je suis 'service'. Je ne connais que ce qui est commandé. Mes supérieurs ils disent toujours 'Avec Jonas on est tranquille'.*

But a character does not have to be a *rough diamond* to speak with a regional accent as most of us do. Look at the characters in the play under study, imagine them with local accents or not, as appropriate, and decide how much you feel the action of the play to be enhanced.

ASSIGNMENTS

1 Select 6 stage directions from a play you have been studying and show how they are intended to affect the audience's involvement and reactions.
2 Give 6 instances from the text of a play to show the level of movement or the lack of it.
3 If music is used to any extent in your play, give examples from the text to show its function.
4 Give 6 examples of the ways in which your playwright maintains the dramatic tension.
5 Show how you think a local dialect might be introduced to good effect into the production of your play.
6 What are the possibilities for audience involvement in your play? Give 6 instances from the text of points in the action where the audience might be brought in.

9

The Poetry Essay

The poetry essay differs radically in certain respects from the other types discussed, since it demands even closer attention to techniques than to themes. It is not so much a question of *what* the poet achieves as *how* (s)he does so. The finished effect will be achieved by use, skilful or otherwise, of metre, intonation, rhyme, alliteration assonance, original imagery, musicality and other devices.

Because also of the peculiar ability of poetry to achieve an emotional response in the listener-reader, the poet will often be trying to reach us via our feelings. However high our own intellectualism, the fundamental appeal of most poetry is to the senses, and we respond to the powerful combination of sounds and pictures offered in any good poem. Therefore we will frequently be looking for the effect of a particular choice of a word, or of a combination of words, or of a stylistic device.

Let us concentrate on the implications of the poet's technique, since the material practised in many of the other chapters in this book will help you with the other aspects of the poetry essay. First, we need to look at the types of question set by the Examining Boards. These may be divided roughly into two groups:

Group A
1 Do you find anything in the work of ... which is relevant to the modern reader?
2 Which poem or group of poems by ... has made the greatest impression on you?
3 Compare and contrast the views of society expressed in the following poems by ... and ...
4 In what sense is ...'s poetry a reaction against the times?
5 Discuss ...'s treatment of the theme of ... in his poetry.
6 Trace the main developments in French poetry since 1850.

Group B
1 From the poetry in your selection, choose any two poems on a common theme and discuss the writer's treatment of it.
2 Based on your reading of the poems in the collection, what evidence is there for considering ... ... and ... to belong to a recognizable poetic movement?
3 How far is poem A or poem B characteristic of its author?
4 Where, in your opinion, do ...'s strengths and weaknesses as a poet lie?

5 Discuss the characteristic features of . . .'s response to death/nature/night/
society. Make detailed reference to at least four poems.
6 Which poet in the collection has had the greatest appeal for you and for
what reasons?

In Group A we are concerned principally with themes, and points of style,
though important, are likely to take second place.

In Group B, however, the emphasis will be at least as much on questions of
style, method and technique, as on themes. Thus, essays on this type of question
should contain much more of a balance between the analysis of ideas and the
means of conveying them.

If the topic on which you have to write falls into category B, then you may
find it easier to organize your material into two separate sections, one dealing
with thematic points, the other with stylistic items. You may also find it easier to
deal with themes and general implications first and to analyse the poet's style in
the latter stages of your essay, much after the manner of the strong treatment
referred to in Chapter 3.

POETIC DEVICES

In order to analyse a poet's style and to make valid comments upon it, you need
to be able to identify the various concrete elements from which a poem is built-
up. Once you can do this, it is not too difficult to pinpoint the particular quality
of a poet's work with a fair degree of accuracy.

Study the list of devices below and look for examples of them in the poems
you have been studying during your course.

EXTERNAL SHAPES

The Alexandrine

The Alexandrine, a twelve-syllable line, has been the standard metre of much of
French poetry. These are variations on the basic pattern, which is called the
Classical Alexandrine. Here, there is a sense-pause called a caesura exactly in the
middle of the line [i.e. after *six* syllables] e.g.:

> Ainsi, toujours poussés|vers de nouveaux rivages,
> Dans la nuit éternelle|emportés sans retour
> > Lamartine: *Le Lac*

In the *Romantic Alexandrine*, there are two caesurae [after the fourth and
eighth syllable] e.g.:

> Où les vaisseaux,|glissant dans l'or|et dans la moire
> > Baudelaire: *La Chevelure*

In *irregular Alexandrines*, the caesura begins to have a will of its own and,
theoretically, may occur almost anywhere. Most frequently, it is found after the
fifth or seventh syllable, e.g.:

> Fileur éternel|des immobilités bleues
> > Rimbaud: *Bateau ivre*

Modern poets make much less use of the Alexandrine than did their predecessors, because of the restrictions it imposes.

Alternation of rhymes [Alternance des rimes]
Until the revolution in poetry towards the end of the nineteenth century, there were strict conventions governing rhyming patterns, especially in relation to poems written in Alexandrines. There follows a very basic explanation of French rhyme.

Feminine rhyme
A feminine line ends in a *mute* -e/-es/-ent.
A feminine rhyme occurs when two feminine lines follow each other, e.g.

> Oh! combien de marins, combien de capitaines
> Qui sont partis joyeux pour des courses lointaines,

Hugo: *Oceano Nox*

Masculine rhyme
Any line which does not terminate in a mute ending is said to be masculine. A masculine rhyme occurs when two masculine lines follow each other, e.g.

> Ni l'entretien d'Adam et d'Ève sur les fleurs,
> Ni le divin sommeil après tant de douleurs;

Leconte de Lisle: *Solvet seclum*

A basic principle of Alexandrine poetry was that a feminine rhyme should be followed by a masculine one and vice-versa. Thus

> Quarante ans sont passés, et ce coin de la terre,
> Waterloo, ce plateau funèbre et solitaire,
> Ce champ sinistre où Dieu mêla tant de néants,
> Tremble encor d'avoir vu la fuite des géants

Hugo: *L'Expiation*

may be said to follow a *regular Alexandrine* rhyming pattern.

Outside of the regular Alexandrine, *rimes croisées* occur when masculine and feminine lines are alternated, producing an *abab* rhyming pattern, e.g.

> Maintenant que du deuil qui m'a fait l'âme obscure
>   Je sors, pâle et vainqueur,
> Et que je sens la paix de la grande nature
>   Qui m'entre dans le cœur

Hugo: *À Villequier*

Rimes embrassées occur when masculine and feminine lines are written in an *abba* rhyming pattern, e.g.

> Voici venir les temps où vibrant sur sa tige
> Chaque fleur s'évapore ainsi qu'un encensoir;
> Les sons et les parfums tournent dans l'air du soir;
> Valse mélancolique et langoureux vertige!

Baudelaire: *Harmonie du soir*

You will sometimes encounter the terms *rimes riches* and *rimes suffisantes*. These have nothing to do with the alternation of rhymes. A *rime riche* is simply one in which the rhyming vowels *and* the consonants immediately preceding and following them are identical, e.g.:

> Mon chat sur le carreau cherchant une litière
> Agite sans repos son corps maigre et galeux;
> L'âme d'un vieux poète erre dans la gouttière
> Avec la triste voix d'un fantôme frileux
>
> Baudelaire: *Spleen*

In a *rime suffisante*, only *one* identical consonant is required, e.g.

> Là, tout n'est qu'ordre et beauté,
> Luxe, calme et volupté
>
> Baudelaire: *L'invitation au voyage*

In *rimes mêlées*, the lines rhyme haphazardly, e.g.:

> Il s'arrête pile devant le patron
> Trois paysans passeront et vous paieront
> Puis disparaît dans le soleil
> Sans régler les consommations
> Disparaît dans le soleil tout en continuant sa chanson.
>
> Jacques Prévert: *Et la fête continue . . .*

Le vers libre is a late nineteenth-century reaction to what was felt to be the excessively rigid structure of classical and establishment poetry. The only real basis of poetic form was felt to be rhythm. Restraints of line and rhyme were swept away. Much modern poetry continues to follow this free pattern, e.g.:

> Debout devant le zinc
> Sur le coup de dix heures
> Un grand plombier zingueur
> Habillé en dimanche et pourtant c'est lundi
> Chante pour lui tout seul
>
> Jacques Prévert: *Et la fête continue . . .*

Rimes suivies follow a straightforward pattern [such as AA BB CC DD EE] of independent rhyming couplets, e.g.:

> J'ai plus de souvenirs que si j'avais mille ans.
> Un gros meuble à tiroirs encombré de bilans,
> De vers, de billets doux, de procès, de romances,
> Avec de lourds cheveux roulés dans des quittances,
> Cache moins de secrets que mon triste cerveau.
> C'est une pyramide, un immense caveau,
>
> Baudelaire: *Spleen*

Terza rima

In this measure, the poet writes his/her lines [usually Alexandrines] in groups of three, with the following rhyming pattern:

> aba bcb cdc ded efe, etc.

The middle line of each tercet rhymes with the first and third lines of the following stanza. It is most commonly used by Théophile Gautier.

> Quand Michel-Ange eut peint la chapelle Sixtine,
> Et que de l'échafaud, sublime et radieux,
> Il fut redescendu dans la cité latine,

> Il ne pouvait baisser ni les bras ni les yeux;
> Ses pieds ne savaient pas comment marcher sur terre;
> Il avait oublié le monde dans les cieux.

> *[Terza rima]*

The sonnet

The French sonnet follows similar patterns to those of its English equivalent. It is basically a 14-line poem consisting of two 4-line and two 3-line stanzas, rhyming ABBA, ABBA, CCD $\left\{ \begin{array}{c} \text{EDE} \\ \text{EED} \end{array} \right\}$.

There are, however, many irregular forms.

Vers impairs

Vers impairs are lines made up of an odd number of syllables. Normally, the ear is accustomed to scanning lines which are even. Consequently, verses consisting of 5, 7, 9, 11 syllables have a tendency to shake the ear out of its usual complacency. Often, they are especially useful for conveying states of feeling, as in Baudelaire's *L'invitation au voyage*, where they help express the poet's dream of a state of intermingled tranquillity, enchantment and voluptuousness.

> Tout y parlerait
> À l'âme en secret
> Sa douce langue natale.

Irregular line length

In the later stages of the nineteenth century, there was a very strong reaction against the limitations on line-length and metre imposed by the classical school of poetry. The ultimate consequence has been the refusal of modern poets to accept any restrictions on the way they build their poems.

In much of the poetry you may read from the period 1870–1900, an irregular line-length will be used occasionally or more frequently for special effect. In this extract from *Réponse à un acte d'accusation*, Victor Hugo uses an irregular line, to emphasize his outcry against the Classicists:

> ... j'ouvris
> Les yeux sur la nature et sur l'art, l'idiome,
> Peuple et noblesse, était l'image du royaume;
> La poésie la monarchie; un mot
> Était un duc et pair, on n'était qu'un grimaud;

Ballad form

There are two regular types of ballad. These are:

(a) A poem of three ten-lined stanzas, each line containing ten syllables, plus a concluding short stanza [an *envoi*] of five lines. The rhyming-pattern is: (ababbccdcd) × 3 + ccdcd.
(b) A poem of three eight-lined stanzas, each line containing eight syllables, plus a concluding short stanza of four lines. The rhyming-pattern is: (ababbcbc) × 3 + bcbc.

ASSIGNMENTS

1 Choose any half-dozen poems from your collection and write down which versification pattern each follows, i.e. is it a regular Alexandrine/sonnet, etc.?
2 Write down the rhyming-pattern for each poem.

INTERNAL DEVICES

Because of the relative lack of a tonic stress in French pronunciation and of the tendency of the language to run words into a smooth flow, poets will resort to the effects achieved by individual words and by the placing together of words which do not flow smoothly in order to produce harder, harsher, more jerky and more distinctive rhythms, e.g.:

Assis nonchalamment súr ún nóir páléfrói
Qui marchait revétu dé hóussés vióléttes

In this extract from *Le Cor*, de Vigny has achieved a jogging rhythm to mirror the trotting of the horse. Note, incidentally, that he has broken the Alexandrine after *marchait* to add to the rhythmic effect.

Assonance

This is a form of internal rhyme where the same or similar vowel sounds are heard several times. Like alliteration [a.v.] with which it is often combined, it is a device which can be used to provide a range of subtle or obvious effects. For example, in *Clair de Lune*, Verlaine employs similar, repeated nasal vowels and long 'a's' to create a world of melodious nostalgia:

Votre âme est un paysage choisi
Que vont charmant masques et bergamasques,
Jouant du luth, et dansant, et quasi
Tristes sous leurs déguisements fantasques.

Alliteration

This is a form of internal rhyme, where the line(s) contain(s) a noticeable frequency of the same or related [c-g, p-b, t-d] consonants. The device occurs commonly, because it is supple enough to provide almost any effect, depending on the particular qualities of the consonants used, e.g.:

D'un *l*arge coup de *l*angue i*l* se *l*ustre *l*a patte;
...
*F*aisant mouvoir sa queue et *f*rissonner ses *f*lancs,

Leconte de Lisle: Le Rêve du jaguar

In this extract the 'l's' convey a licking sound and the 'f's' suggest the tremendous energy stored inside the jaguar.

Open vowels

These are the vowels which are not nasalized, or used in combination. Consequently, they have a more open, clear quality and may be used to slow down the pace of the lines, or to give them a sonorous, stately quality, as in:

M*i*d*i*, roi d*e*s ét*é*s, *é*pand*u* s*u*r l*a* plaine

Leconte de Lisle: Midi

Enjambement

Enjambement occurs when a sense grouping of words reaches beyond the end of one line into the first words of the next. It can be used to create a variety of effects such as a rushing flow of thoughts or events, or, as in the example below, an impression of a far-reaching country landscape.

L'échelonnement des haies
Moutonne à l'infini, mer
Claire dans le brouillard clair

Verlaine: L'Échelonnement des haies

The word(s) necessary to complete the sense of the preceding line [in our example, 'moutonne' and 'claire'] is/are known as the *rejet*.

End-stopping

This term simply means the occurrence of a punctuation mark at the end of a line. Such marks are nothing more than a written means of indicating breath-pauses. Thus, when a stanza is heavily end-stopped, the pace of the poem is slowed-down, e.g.:

Midi, roi des étes, épandu sur la plaine,
 Tombe en nappes d'argent des hauteurs du ciel.
Tout se tait. L'air flamboie et brûle sans haleine;
La terre est assoupie en sa robe de feu.

Leconte de Lisle: Midi

Listing

This device is used principally for climax/emphasis and/or to stimulate the listener's imagination, e.g.:

Voici la verte Écosse et la brune Italie,
Et la Grèce, ma mère, où le miel est si doux,
Argos, et Ptéléon, ville des hécatombes;
Et Messa, la divine, agréable aux colombes;
Et le front chevelu du Pélion changeant;

In this extract from *La Nuit de Mai*, Musset has used a list of evocative place-names to conjure up impressions of sunlight and exotic, distant lands.

Rhetorical questions

These are questions which know what answer to expect and are used for effect, rather than simply to elicit a specific answer, e.g.:

> Âmes des Chevaliers, revenez-vous encor?
> Est-ce vous qui parlez avec la voix du Cor?
>
> Alfred de Vigny: *Le Cor*

Here, de Vigny is using the rhetorical question almost as a fanfare to introduce the story of the noble Roland.

Apostrophe

Apostrophe is an exclamatory and usually [highly] rhetorical address to a person, place, animal or phenomenon, who or which is often one of the central concerns of the poem. This device is particularly common in nineteenth-century poetry, but is used nonetheless effectively by modernists such as Georges Moustaki, here conducting a one-sided conversation with the mother of every twenty year old girl:

> Chacun de ses vingt ans pour vous a compté double
> Vous connaissez déjà tout ce qu'elle découvre
> Vous avez oublié les choses qui la troublent
> Madame
> Et vous troublaient aussi.
>
> [*Votre fille a vingt ans, Madame*]

Banality

All poets, including the greatest, are capable of writing lines, stanzas and even whole poems, which are so banal and commonplace as to be scarcely worth reading. So try not to fall into the trap of thinking that because a particular poem has been written by a poet of repute, everything in it must be good. Take, for instance, these lines from Hugo's *Lorsque l'enfant paraît* ...

> Vous êtes parmi nous la colombe de l'arche.
> Vos pieds tendres et purs n'ont point l'âge où l'on marche,
>   Vos ailes sont d'azur.

The kindest thing one might say about them is that they are uninspired.

Cacophony

The literal meaning of *cacophony* is *discordant sound* and the device is used by a poet when (s)he wants to assault the listener's ear, by the harsh quality of the sound, e.g.

> Un *frigidaire*
> Un joli *scooter*

Un *atomixer*
Et du *Dunlopillo*

Boris Vian: *Complainte du progrès*

Here, Vian plays on the harsh or even foreign quality in the names of the inventions. The abruptness with which they impinge upon the ear gives an impression both of the pop-pop motion of the scooter and of society's progress.

POETIC STYLE AND THE USE OF POETIC DEVICES

It is now time to look at what we may write about the ways in which a poet uses the various elements from which a poem may be built up.

The first point to remember is the fact that many people find essays on poetic style difficult to write, since there is a great temptation to over-generalize. When you are writing about a poet's style and methods, be absolutely specific. Break down the poems and define the invidual themes and devices used.

Here is a check-list of the broad points for which you should be looking.

POETIC STYLE CHECK-LIST

1 *Favourite or specific themes*

2 *Verse forms*
  Type of stanza
  Type of line
  Length of line
  Variation/irregularity in line
  Rhythm of the line
  Odd number of syllables
  If sonnet, regular/irregular?
  Incidence of mute e's

3 *Rhyme*
  Type of rhyme
  Predominance of *rimes riches*?
  Predominance of *rimes suffisantes*?
  Effect of the blend of these rhymes
  Effect of *rimes faibles*?
  Internal rhyme – assonance and alliteration
  Does the sound mirror the sense?

4 *Nature of vocabulary*
  Simple/elaborate?
  Concrete/abstract?
  Emotive/sensuous?
  Good choice of word – clear vivid picture?
  Evocative proper names?
  Exotic images?

Chosen for sound as well as meaning?
Popular expression?
Invented words?

5 *Figures of speech*
Metaphors and similes are they
striking/illuminating/original/
rich in meaning and association/
trite/overdone/far-fetched/
ambiguous/ridiculous?
Antithesis – is it dramatic?
Personification – more vivid presentation of idea?
Repetition – for dramatic or musical effect?
Apostrophe/rhetorical questions?
Climax?
Enumeration?

As we have already agreed, it is so easy to be nebulous when writing about poetry. You have been exhorted to be specific! The check-list will undoubtedly help you towards that goal. Of further help, the sample writing below, shows a variety of essayists, all making highly specific points, tied down to concrete, short textual reference.

(a) Lamartine, as an elegiac poet, finds the predictable rise and fall of the regular Alexandrine best suited to his poetry. In *Le Lac*, however, he chooses to vary the pattern, with the frequent interspersion of six-syllable lines, which have the effect of lengthening the fluent melody of the stanza and of highlighting the most crucial thought:

> 'Tu mugissais ainsi sous ces roches profondes;
> Ainsi tu te brisais sur leurs flancs déchirés;
> Ainsi le vent jetait l'écume de tes ondes
>   *Sur les pieds adorés.*'

The sonority of the first three lines in this stanza reflects the power of the natural forces which are unleashed and leads to the climax of the last line, where our attention is held by the contrasting image. It is also worth noting how the visual impression of the shorter line on paper adds to its significance.

(b) In *Clair de lune*, Verlaine adds to the melodiousness by using rhymes that are mostly rich; many of them formed on open vowel sounds:

> 'un paysage *choisi*, bergam*asques*, et *quasi*, fant*asques*'.

Such sounds are richly evocative of past times in this context.

(c) Verlaine employs a similar device in *Chanson d'Automne* to evoke a state of nostalgia. The rhyme vowels of the first two stanzas are predominantly nasal, unlike the brisk open vowels of the last stanza which evokes a brusque change of mood. Nasal vowels linger in the air, as our thoughts linger in the past:

'Tout suffoc*ant*
Et blême, qu*and*

→

Sonne l'heure,
Je me souvi*ens*
Des jours anci*ens*
Et je pleure:'

(d) It is a common device to associate old age with an autumnal scene. To mirror the quietude of this stage in life in *La Vigne*, Lamartine makes subtle use of the mute 'e', as well as of assonance and alliteration:

'Cet*te* heur*e* a pour nos *s*en*s* des impre*ss*ions douc*es*
Co*mm*e des pas *mu*ets qui *m*ar*ch*ent *s*ur des *m*ou*ss*es.'

The soft sibilants in words such as '*s*en*s*, impre*ss*ions, *s*ur, mou*ss*es' re-inforce the feeling that this is a time for reflection.

(e) Typical of Laforgue's style is his need to express aggression, if not to shock. These feelings he often renders by his characteristic use of cacophony, as in the final stanza of *Encore un livre*:

'J'ai|fait|mon|*t*emps|, je *d*éguer*p*is
Vers l'In*cl*usive Sinécure.'

If he is to go, he will go, but he retains some of his defiance in the way he makes the sounds fall almost blow by blow. '*L*'in*cl*usive Sinécure' is indeed cacophonous and his mood is supported by the separation of 'J'ai|fait|mon|temps'. The blunt determination telegraphs the message that he is no easy victim.

(f) One should not look for original simile and metaphor in Lamartine's work. Characteristic of his vocabulary are words such as 'profond, lointain, charme, serein, obscure, molle clarté', suggesting the quiet delight taken by the poet in living, nature, memory and in gentle melancholy.

(g) In *La Maison du Berger*, de Vigny develops the not very original metaphor of the enchained heart in parallel with the image of a galley in mourning

'Si *ton âme enchaînée*, ainsi que l'est mon âme,
Lasse de son boulet et de son *pain amer*,
Sur sa galère en deuil laisse tomber la rame,'

Personally, I find the italicized material most trite, but fortunately de Vigny produces much more original imagery in the course of the poem.

Group A

As far as these types of essay are concerned, you will find help with isolating and setting out your points in other chapters (especially pages 15, 22 and 77). You should have little trouble developing your essay, since you are principally concerned with themes.

However, what we have discussed in relation to work on poetic style, will still be relevant to your writing, since (a) you will need to be specific in your highlighting of points and in your use of quotation and (b) style cannot be totally divorced from theme. If you take a theme, say, the city environment, you need to show *how* the poet develops it and this will inevitably require reference to individual lines and stylistic devices.

Below are example paragraphs relating to the treatment of themes:

(h) Lamartine is justifiably regarded as one of the most lyrical of French poets. His principal themes are love, nature, God and the family. For him, love is spiritualized and idealized into an ethereal emotion. There is a consequent reluctance to describe the object of his love together with the suppression of physical elements, as in *L'Isolement*:

> 'Et ce bien idéal que toute âme désire,
> Et qui n'a pas de nom au terrestre séjour.'

His attitude towards love could hardly be purer. In these lines there is the implication that through our earthly love we come to glimpse the nature of Heaven.

(i) Despite his modernity as a poet, Boris Vian treats the same themes that have occupied poets through the centuries. His anti-war poems follow in the tradition of folk songs such as *Le Conscrit du Languedoc*, his concern for the urban environment shows a close affinity with Baudelaire, and his confrontation of old age and death in *Le Crâne*, echoes any number of predecessors:

> 'Et puis je n'aurai plus
> Ce phosphore un peu mou
> Cerveau qui me servit
> À me prévoir sans vie
> Les osses tout verts'.

What is different is the lightness of the line and the indications of self-mockery in the almost punning 'cerveau qui me servit'.

ASSIGNMENTS

1 Match each critical comment with the correct quotation.

    i Jetant shakos, manteaux, fusils, jetant les aigles

    ii On prendra le tram trente-trois

    iii Une ondulation majestueuse et lente
       S'éveille, et va mourir à l'horizon poudreux

    iv Voici le troupeau roux des tordeuses de hanches:
       Soyez fous, vous serez drôles, étant hagards!

    v Mon enfant, ma soeur,
      Songe à la douceur
      D'aller là-bas vivre ensemble!

(a) The isolation of individual words and the deliberate breaking of the line produce an awkward rolling motion.

(b) Here, the enjambement is used to considerable effect. The *rejet* stands out and underlines the impression of a briefly envigorating awakening.

(c) In this deceptively simple single line, Jacques Brel uses both assonance and alliteration to create an effect of exhilaration and hurly-burly.

(d) The poet uses listing and climax to convey the defeated army's feelings of bitterness, frustration and desperation.

(e) Not only does the poet use an impair line to convey a state of feeling, but he lengthens every third line, to create a regular point of return and security after the spontaneous flight of the couplet.

2 For each passage choose the correct completion for the critical comment.

(a) Ce vieillard possédait des champs de blés et d'orge;
Il était, quoique riche, à la justice enclin;
Il n'avait pas de fange en l'eau de son moulin,
Il n'avait pas d'enfer dans le feu de sa forge.

(Hugo: *Booz endormi*)

(b) Longtemps au pied du perron de
La maison où entra la dame
Que j'avais suivie pendant deux
Bonnes heures à Amsterdam
Mes doigts jetèrent des baisers.

(Apollinaire: *Rosemonde*)

(c) Votre âme est un paysage choisi
Que vont charmant masques et bergamasques
Jouant du luth, et dansant, et quasi
Tristes sous leurs déguisements fantasques.

(Verlaine: *Clair de Lune*)

(d) Va cueillir des remords dans la fête servile,
Ma Douleur, donne-moi la main; viens par ici.

(Baudelaire: *Recueillement*)

(e) Oh combien de marins, combien de capitaines
Qui sont partis joyeux pour des courses lointaines
Dans ce morne horizon se sont évanouis!
Combien ont disparu, dure et triste fortune!

(Hugo: *Oceano Nox*)

(a) The balance of the line and the august, revered nature of the personality are reinforced by the poet's frequent use of
  i end-stopping
  ii apostrophe
  iii cacophony
  iv a jogging rhythm

(b) This extract might be described as one long
  i apostrophe

    ii rhetorical question
    iii *terza rima*
    iv enjambement
in which Guillaume Apollinaire rushes us along to the vital point of the stanza to be found in the last words.
(c) The
    i *rimes croisées*
    ii regular alexandrines
    iii romantic alexandrines
    iv *vers impairs*
are well-suited to the general atmosphere of nostalgia.
(d) The poet uses
    i frequent end-stopping
    ii rimes riches
    iii bathos
    iv enjambement
to increase the sense of personal urgency.
(e) The
    i light, airy sounds
    ii sonority of the vowels
    iii antithesis
    iv personification
complements the rhythm and adds to the impression of a rising and falling motion so appropriate to the subject.

3 Use the check-list on page 71 as a basis and make notes on the verse forms of the poems in your collection.

4 Use Section 3 of the check-list and analyse the types of rhyme used by your poet(s).

5 Take any one or two poems by *one* poet and, using Section 4 of the check-list to help you, make notes on the vocabulary used.

6 Work through your collection of poems and find examples of as many different figures of speech as possible.

7 Using examples (a)–(i) as a guide, select an important 1–5 line quote from each of your poems and write a short paragraph of commentary on it.

8 Isolate and make notes on the separate themes which occupy your poet(s).

9 Compare and contrast the treatment of a similar theme in two poems.

10 Take any one of the topics in Group A on page 63, fill in the gap(s) to suit your author and draw up a rough draft for an essay.

11 Do the same with any Group B topic on pages 63–64.

10

The Context Question

Many students try to avoid context questions, because they are afraid of them and tend to see them as a trap. They think that the question has been set simply as a difficult memory test, requiring a very exact identification of a passage and not much more.

It will help you to feel easier about this type of literary assignment, if you can accept that it has a more creative purpose than simply to force students into working at a book, head down, trying to memorize the lay-out of the work.

WHAT IS THE CONTEXT QUESTION?

It is not a translation exercise or an opportunity to tell the story. Part of its intention, admittedly, is to discover whether you have read the work thoroughly, but it also attempts to find out whether you have read it with understanding and whether you have the ability to analyse a small and often highly significant piece of text.

Therefore, if you have made a mistake in locating a passage, take heart! You may still be able to do quite well with the question as a whole, if your general understanding and analysis of the passage are of a good standard.

HOW SHOULD ONE SET ABOUT TACKLING A CONTEXT QUESTION?

It is just as well to ask this, since Examination Boards often give you little guidance as to how to structure your answer. Others, however, are helpfully specific.

Generally speaking, you will not go far wrong if you divide your answer into the following four sections:

1 Identifying the location of the passage;
2 A commentary on the passage;
3 The significance of the passage;
4 Points of special interest.

LOCATING THE PASSAGE

Since the title of the assignment is the *context* question, it is possible to develop a fixation about this section of your answer and to go to *great lengths* to complete it. However, it is not necessary to write at *great length* about where the passage (or whole poem) occurs in the work.

On the contrary, your answer is likely to be all the better for an economical statement of where the extract occurs.

2 A COMMENTARY ON THE PASSAGE

This is a trap for the unwary. It is not an exercise in translation or paraphrasing. You are required to work through the passage, analysing the meaning of the lines in relation to the work as a whole. Page 82 gives a clear example of this procedure. Note how it avoids giving a word-for-word translation of every line, but picks up, instead, their significance for the characters, for their roles, and for the conclusion of the play.

3 THE SIGNIFICANCE OF THE PASSAGE

Here, you comment on the relevance of the extract to the work as a whole. Start by asking yourself *Why was this passage chosen?* Does it:

    (a) encapsulate main themes?
    (b) reflect the author's aims and concerns?
    (c) occur at a vital stage?
    (d) affect the reader (audience) strongly?
    (e) present the author at his (her) best/worst?
    (f) present a typical example of the author's style?

4 POINTS OF SPECIAL INTEREST

These may relate to:

    (a) the author's style
    (b) (auto)biographical detail
    (c) historical detail
    (d) parallel work by other authors
    (e) topical reference.

THE POETRY CONTEXT QUESTION

This has somewhat different requirements from the other two *genres*, since, with poetry, you have to look for a large number of specific points. Below is a check-list of the points.

POETRY CONTEXT CHECK-LIST

Section A Placing the passage in its context

    1 Give the name of the poem, the poet and the collection from which it comes (e.g. *Les Fleurs du Mal, Sagesse, Alcools, Cantilènes en gelée.*)

2 State at which point in the poem the extract occurs.
3 Say how it fits into the general structure.
4 State very briefly (in one sentence) if it is typical of the poet's attitude (to poetry, nature, love, religion, society, his/her own life) and whether it can be related to his or her background or experience.

Section B The theme of the passage

5 State briefly in your own words the theme of the passage.
6 Do not paraphrase.
7 Give the basic idea, pointing out the key line(s) or stanza.
8 Show how this basic idea or emotion is amplified and illustrated by the rest of the extract.
9 Comment very briefly on the clarity or otherwise of the statement of the idea.

Section C Comment on the style of the passage

10 Comment on the figures of speech used.
11 Comment on the nature of the vocabulary, especially on the choice of verbs, adjectives and adverbs.
12 State whether the vocabulary is simple or elaborate, concrete or abstract, emotive or sensuous. Is there a good choice of individual words, giving a clear, vivid picture? Is there any use of colourful, evocative proper names? Are words chosen for their sound as well as for their meaning?
Are the similes and metaphors original and striking? Are they illuminating? Do they contain a wealth of meaning and of associations? Are they far-fetched? Ridiculous? Trite?
Is there any use of (dramatic) antithesis? [e.g. *On était vaincu par sa conquête.*]
Is personification used. If so, does it present ideas more vividly?
How much repetition is there? Is it used for dramatic or musical effect?
Is there any use made of other devices such as climax, enumeration, apostrophe?
13 What is the effect of the rhythm? Is there a musical quality? Describe the rhythm briefly. Is it smooth or broken, slow or rapid, etc.? What use is made of open or closed vowels?
14 Refer to the verse-form used by the poet. Comment on the type of stanza, the length of line, the rhythm [which depends upon the number of *trimetres* (Roman Alexandrines)], enjambement, variation in line-length, number of mute 'e''s, lines with an odd number of syllables. Is the poem a sonnet and is it regular or irregular?
15 Refer to the rhyme, its type, the predominance of *rimes riches* and their effect. Similarly what is the effect of the *rimes faibles?*
16 How much use has been made of assonance and alliteration. In short, how far does the sound of the poem correspond to its sense?

There is a considerable amount of material to be covered here and when you have a very finite amount of time at your disposal to answer an exam question (usually an hour at most), it is unlikely you will be able to deal with every item in the above list. Therefore, you will have to judge for yourself your priorities (as has occurred in the sample answer on page 84). Some material may have to be left out and your own order of listing will vary from the above.

ASSIGNMENT

Read the sample context answers which follow, note the strategies used, consult with your teacher, choose suitable passages in your own set books and attempt your answers, following the headings given in the samples.

LE GRAND MEAULNES

Jusqu'au jeudi suivant le temps resta à la pluie. Et ce jeudi-là fut plus triste encore que le précédent. Toute la campagne était baignée dans une sorte de brume glacée comme aux plus mauvais jours de l'hiver.

Millie, trompée par le beau soleil de l'autre semaine, avait fait faire la lessive, mais il ne fallait pas songer à mettre sécher le linge sur les haies du jardin, ni même sur des cordes dans le grenier, tant l'air était humide et froid.

En discutant avec M. Seurel, il lui vint l'idée d'étendre sa lessive dans les classes, puisque c'était jeudi, et de chauffer le poêle à blanc. Pour économiser les feux de la cuisine et de la salle à manger, on ferait cuire les repas sur le poêle et nous nous tiendrions toute la journée dans la grande salle du Cours.

Au premier instant – j'étais si jeune encore – je considérai cette nouveauté comme une fête.

Morne fête! ... Toute la chaleur du poêle était prise par la lessive et il faisait grand froid. Dans la cour, tombait interminablement et mollement une petite pluie d'hiver. C'est là pourtant que dès neuf heures du matin, dévoré d'ennui, je retrouvai le Grand Meaulnes.

The location of the passage

The extract is taken from the concluding stages of Part Two of *Le Grand Meaulnes*. Several months after his discovery of the *domaine mystérieux*, Meaulnes decides to leave for Paris. These paragraphs lead up to the moment when he will inform François of his decision.

A commentary on the passage

Alain-Fournier sets the atmosphere for Augustin Meaulnes' announcement by emphasizing the demoralizing nature of the weather. The rain brings melancholy and this is reflected in the icy fogginess of the landscape, so reminiscent of winter and death.

The prevailing atmosphere of insecurity within the novel is maintained by the accumulation of mundane detail, relating to Millie's concern with the washing. The winter weather has flattered only to deceive in its proverbial manner, so even Millie's domestic plans are thwarted. The tediousness is developed by the compiling of further rather trivial detail and, behind it, there is the feeling that in such an atmosphere of stultifying ordinariness, Augustin, obsessed with the rediscovery of a magical world somewhere outside the school, will eventually have to break away. Thus, the invasion of the classrooms by the strings of washing to be dried, will find no favour with the escapist Augustin. This fact is subtly underlined by the insistence on the need felt by the teachers to economize on expenditure. This is the antithesis of the world he had discovered at the *château*.

For a moment, the train of the narrative is broken by an emotive comment from the narrator, remembering his childhood, its lost innocence and its sense of wonderment.

But such intervention is not allowed to impinge for long, as, after giving his boyish approval of the small change in school routine, he returns to the theme of oppressive winter. Childish celebration is soon dashed by continued insistence on the mournfulness of the season. In fact, the practical effect of the day's change was to increase the physical discomfort of the pupils by taking their classroom warmth away from them. In the yard, a fine winter drizzle, in itself depressing, has settled in and when François encounters Augustin, the latter is characteristically gnawed by boredom.

The significance of the passage
The passage has been constructed to lead up to Augustin's announcement of a most significant decision. It is typical of those sections of the novel which concentrate on the building up of atmosphere. It is also typical of François' ambivalent memories of life at the family school, transmitting as it does feelings of the security brought about by the child's ordered life in a familiar institution, together with intimations of the repressions felt by the free spirit of adolescence, straining to be away. The oxymoron of *morne fête* characterizes this ambivalence.

Points of special interest
The language is typical of a novel in which the pervading atmosphere is often one of tedium and anxiety. Characteristically, Alain-Fournier uses the natural elements to parallel mental attitudes. The passage is full of references to the inclement season – *reste à la pluie, plus triste, une sorte de brume glacée, tant l'air était humide et froid, il faisait grand froid, tombait interminablement et mollement une petite pluie d'hiver.* Small wonder, then, that François should be *dévoré d'ennui*.

The balanced and measured structure of the sentences reflects almost musically the quiet, unstressed need of captive youth to accept the tedium and strictures of an environment inconducive to imagination or to the flights of fancy:

> *Jusqu'au jeudi suivant le temps resta à la pluie. Et ce jeudi-là fut plus triste encore que le précédent.*

Three short interventions – *Morne fête! J'étais si jeune encore! dévoré d'ennui* – hint at the frustrations of youth and the coming eruption.

LE ROI SE MEURT
MARGUERITE. Des cordes encore t'enlacent que je n'ai pas dénouées. Ou que je n'ai pas coupées. Des mains s'accrochent encore à toi et te retiennent.

Tournant autour du Roi, Marguerite coupe dans le vide, comme si elle avait dans les mains des ciseaux invisibles.

LE ROI. Moi. Moi. Moi.

MARGUERITE. Ce toi n'est pas toi. Ce sont des objets étrangers, des adhérences, des parasites monstrueux. Le gui poussant sur la branche n'est pas la branche, le lierre qui grimpe sur le mur n'est pas le mur. Tu ploies sous le fardeau, tes épaules sont courbées, c'est cela qui te vieillit. Et ces boulets que tu traînes, c'est cela qui entrave ta marche. (*Marguerite se penche, elle enlève des boulets invisibles des pieds du Roi, puis elle se relève en ayant l'air de faire un grand effort pour soulever les boulets.*) Des tonnes, des tonnes, ça pèse des tonnes. (*Elle fait mine de jeter ces boulets en direction de la salle puis se redresse allégée.*) Ouf! Comment as-tu pu traîner cela toute une vie! (*Le Roi essaye de se redresser.*) Je me demandais pourquoi tu étais voûté, c'est à cause de ce sac. (*Marguerite fait mine d'enlever un sac des épaules du Roi et de le jeter.*) Et de cette besace. (*Même geste de Marguerite pour la besace.*) Et de ces godasses de rechange.

LE ROI, *sorte de grognement.* Non.

The location of the passage

The extract is taken from the final stages of *Le Roi se meurt*. Queen Marguerite has worked heroically to prepare Bérenger for his entry into death. With the king and queen alone on stage, Marguerite must free her increasingly frail husband from the last of the heavy burdens which tie him to life.

A commentary on the passage

Marguerite explains to Bérenger that the reason he is finding it so difficult to make his final journey, is the unseen bonds which still tie him to his kingdom and to this earth. The queen, mindful of her responsibility for her husband, carries out a symbolical severing of these links by cutting through the air with a pair of invisible scissors.

Bérenger shows remnants of resistance when he utters *Moi. Moi. Moi,* as if the loosing of the ties has cut into the very stuff of him. His queen is quick to point out that it is not the real him which he is relinquishing, but rather the irrelevant appurtenances one acquires during a lifetime. These acquisitions are nothing more than parasitical growths, frightful in their consequences for the inner man or woman, whom they may obscure and harm like mistletoe on a tree.

These burdensome adhesions age and weigh down his body, and, indeed, his spirit. There are other symbolical impedimenta, such as the balls and chains around his ankles, which, unless he frees himself of them, will prevent him walking to meet his death. Once more, Marguerite fulfils her role as his guiding éminence and mimes the action of removing the prison instruments. For her, it is no easy task because of the weight of the attachments to the world which Bérenger has built up. It is all but too much for her. She comments on their extreme heaviness and wonders, almost rhetorically, how the king can have carried such a burden with him during this life.

As if to underline the validity of her comment, Bérenger attempts to rise and fails. Now Marguerite knows why her husband has become so bowed with age. He needs to be relieved of the still further burdens weighing him down and she removes from him his invisible bag, pilgrim's satchel and spare shoes, all themselves symbolical of a journey through life.

Bérenger is now too weak to utter much more than a feeble protest, but the grunted *Non* is enough to indicate that he is still attached to the things of this world which he has acquired.

The significance of the passage
The extract is a key to an understanding of the play as a whole, underlining as it does the central theme of *Le Roi se meurt* – man's need to prepare himself for the leaving of this world, and, in so doing, to make some sense of his existence. It occurs at an important point, when Marguerite is obliged to make great physical efforts to sustain Bérenger during his final journey. Had she failed him here, then he would not have been able to take the last, tottering steps into death, of his own accord.

The passage is typical of Ionesco in the way he uses mime to convey symbolical action. Marguerite's efforts, stripped of the distraction of actual physical objects, are conveyed to the audience in their essential simplicity. In so doing, they mirror mankind's need to attain to an understanding of the simple facts of our condition, facts which lie obscured by the many attachments to this life, which we build up during the living of it.

In addition to conveying the stark, straightforward nature of Bérenger's state, the mime, like all good mime, generates a sympathetic response.

This extract, with its elements of clarity, its dramatic involvement and its implicit pathos, represents the best of Ionesco's theatre.

Points of special interest
There is a high emotional charge in this passage. It reflects very closely the crisis in Ionesco's own life, when his serious illness caused him to deliberate at length on the question of the individual's preparation for death. In a very real sense, the play is the dramatized result of that deliberation.

The extract conveys an impression of the highly visual nature of Ionesco's theatre and, although we are not here faced with the most obvious effects of *lourdeur*, such as increasing cracks in the masonry and concertina-ing walls, the large amount of mime is a reminder of the playwright's concern that the poignancy of our often absurd condition should be communicated strongly.

The style of the language in the passage is familiar, at times extremely familiar in the context of our stereotyped conception of royalty – *ça pèse des tonnes, godasses de rechange*. This reflects Ionesco's belief that life is too vital a process for it to be obscured by the veils of formal language.

L'INVITATION AU VOYAGE

Mon enfant, ma soeur,
Songe à la douceur
D'aller là-bas vivre ensemble!
Aimer à loisir,
Aimer et mourir

Au pays qui te ressemble!
    Les soleils mouillés
    De ces ciels brouillés
Pour mon esprit ont les charmes
    Si mystérieux
    De tes traîtres yeux,
Brillant à travers leurs larmes.

Là, tout n'est qu'ordre et beauté,
Luxe, calme et volupté.

    Des meubles luisants,
    Polis par les ans,
Décoreraient notre chambre;
    Les plus rares fleurs
    Mêlant leurs odeurs
Aux vagues senteurs de l'ambre,
    Les riches plafonds,
    Les miroirs profonds,
La splendeur orientale,
    Tout y parlerait
    À l'âme en secret
Sa douce langue natale.

Là, tout n'est qu'ordre et beauté,
Luxe, calme et volupté.

The location of the passage

The extract is the first two of the three sections which make up Baudelaire's poem *L'invitation au voyage*, from the collection, *Spleen et Idéal*. The first stanza and couplet conjure up the world of the poet's beloved, the second section takes us into its exotic charms and the final section, not included in the extract, takes us into a Dutch landscape, another part of the world of his woman. *Le voyage* is an example of the theme of escape, so frequently found in Baudelaire's poetry, an escape from the mundane world into the fulfilment of the senses.

The main theme

The poet finds his passions and senses satisfied in the sensual world created by his private contact with the woman of his affections. It is an exclusive world from which everyday cares and acquaintances are banned and in which Baudelaire achieves a state of voluptuous tranquillity. For all its stressing of the senses, it is an oddly passionless poem, as we are reminded by the insistence on *ordre*, *beauté* and *calme* in the repeated couplet refrain.

Much as in *La Chevelure*, the poet is brought into the world of the senses by his contact with and the presence of an idealized woman. This New World is an ordered one, as is conveyed by the precise structure of the poem. The first stanza is a concentration on the general aspects of this world. The second takes us into an oriental exterior, which is expressive of luxury and which is in marked contrast with his present state. When, eventually, in the final section of the poem, we are introduced to a Dutch landscape in the world which resembles the woman, we find that it symbolizes the calm which comes from the fulfilment of the senses.

Both the development within the poem and the imagery are clearly defined, a process which is consistent with an ideal of beauty which is more classical than romantic.

The style of the passage

Baudelaire has created a country of the senses, which is both voluptuous and tranquil. To achieve the effect, he has used a difficult stanza form – 557, 557, 557, 557 and 77. The short lines are particularly suitable for suggesting states of feeling. The rhythms are short but not staccato and, since few of the lines are end-stopped, they allow the landscape to flow on, expressing the poet's dream of an enchanted state. The *impair* metre is an effective vehicle for the impressionistic character of the poem and the shorter lines cause important words and images to stand out in relief:

> Les soleils *mouillés*
> De ces ciels *brouillés*

> Des meubles *luisants*,
> Polis par les *ans*.

The short, *impair* nature of the lines almost forces the poet into suggesting details, rather than painting them in fully. We are given items of colour, such as *meubles luisants, rares fleurs, vagues senteurs, riches plafonds, miroirs profonds, splendeur orientale*, but no attempt is made to dwell upon them. They are scattered lightly in their rich profusion.

This technique is well-suited to Baudelaire's purpose, the symbolizing of a state of perfect love in which the beloved's charms are not detailed, nor are her emotions analysed. Cleverly, his state of feeling towards the woman is suggested by analogy with the sense impressions.
Only in

> *les charmes*
> *Si mystérieux*
> *De tes traîtres yeux*
> *Brillant à travers leurs larmes*

does the poet make specific reference to the physical characteristics of the idealized woman. The remaining comparisons are achieved by suggestion and analogy. Thus, it is the proximity of the *bien aimée* in their private world which conjures up the *vagues senteurs de l'ambre*.

Central to this almost allusive style is the poet's use of assonance. As in *La Chevelure*, he employs nasal vowels to give sonority, a sense of luxury and a feeling of nostalgia to his lines –

> Mêl*ant* leurs odeurs
> Aux vagues s*ent*eurs de l'*ambre*,

> La splendeur orientale
> Tout y parlerait
> *À* l'*âme en* secret
> Sa douce langue natale.

Note also the way in which the long *a*'s in these last two lines seem to lengthen the moment of ecstasy.

As usual with Baudelaire, his choice of individual words and detail is exact and the precision of his language mirrors the ordered, classical beauty which he has created.

For instance, his idealized woman is not simply *mon amour*, or *ma bien-aimée*, but *mon enfant, ma soeur*. The choice of vocabulary conveys feelings of protection and of the need for a lengthy, stable relationship. There is a strong impression of wistfulness here. *Songe* implies at the beginning of the voyage that the discovery cannot last for ever.

When the word *pays* takes us into the extended analogy, we are first presented with details of the New Land, which relate back to the world of everyday reality – *mouillés, brouillés, traîtres*, yet this world is broken by the first statement of the refrain, which insists upon an ordered and reliably peaceful world. Sensuousness is paired with order.

In the luxurious Oriental interior, the soul is suffused with sensation. There are gleaming light, *des meubles luisants*, the colour and the perfume of exotic flowers, mingling with other eastern perfumes, but in this world of escape, the phrase that stands out among the sense impressions is *notre chambre*. It will be our own room and it will satisfy the poet's yearning that

> Tout y parlerait
> À l'âme en secret
> ←
> Sa douce langue natale.

Among all the sensations, it is a calm stability which is sought after, a private, gentle *correspondence*, which will speak the language of the soul, unsullied as at birth by the tedium and repressions of an inimical, ordinary life. How well these lines fit in with the part-pleading insistence of the couplets.

11

The Background Essay

This type of essay has been introduced by certain Examination Boards in recent years and maintained by others over a much longer period in order to allow students some variety in the kinds of answers they write. Apart from providing a change, it is a deliberate attempt to help candidates of a less literary turn of mind, since it allows them to concentrate on the sociological and historical implications of specific books.

But the background essay should not be seen as a soft option for the less well-endowed student, as sometimes happens. For a start, intelligent students do not always have to be literature-minded. This is just as well, since the background question has an intellectual rigour of its own and is as valid as the rest of the material on the paper.

There are two basic types of background essay. These are:

1 topics relating to important people, trends and events from the period studied.
2 Alternative topics of a non-literary nature on the actual set books.

EXAMPLE QUESTIONS

Type 1: Discuss the contribution made by Bergson, Mme. Curie, Le Corbusier or Pasteur to Western society.
Type 2: What do we learn of nineteenth-century social problems from either *Madame Bovary* or *L'Éducation sentimentale*?

When we compare these two types of question, they appear to be looking for very different things. Type 1 seems to require something of a factual narrative on an historical basis, whereas Type 2 requires interpretation of material which you will have had to distil from a literary text.

If this apparent divergence were true, then the straightforward historical narrative would be an easier task than the interpretative analysis. In other words, students attempting Type 2 would be discriminated against, because they were choosing something which was intrinsically more demanding. But Examination Boards would not be foolish enough to allow such an unfair discrepancy. The truth is that Type 1 also requires some interpretation. Notice that the key-word is *discuss*. It might well have been *analyse*.

Let us look at sample paragraphs by two students who have written an essay on Général de Gaulle, in order to clarify the point.

A   *Charles de Gaulle was a great figure in the political and military life of France. He was born in Lille in 1890, gained entry to the famous military academy of Saint-Cyr in 1905 and was wounded three times as a junior officer during the First World War. By the time the next war came, he had been promoted to the rank of commander of one of the tank divisions which were to bear the brunt of the conflict with the German armoured divisions along the Maginot Line and elsewhere.*

B   *One of the many qualities which de Gaulle shared with Churchill was his remarkable degree of foresight, allied to an ability to learn quickly from life's lessons. He never forgot how the État-Major had neglected to build up France's heavy artillery in preparation for the First World War and many of his fellow Saint-Cyriens had been mown down by German artillery, as they mounted a series of anachronistic cavalry charges for lack of any more up-to-date means of attack. Thus, when the Maginot Line, brain-child of Marshal Pétain, was constructed during the 1930s to ward off any further German aggression, he spoke out almost alone against the line. He saw that Pétain and his followers had taken no account of the advances made in tank and aviation technology. Rightly, like Churchill exhorting his own country to re-arm effectively, he foresaw a repetition of the sweeping German advances of 1914.*

It is easy to see why B will score much more highly than A. She has made a very worthwhile attempt to see beyond the basic facts and to assess their implications. There is real interpretation here. On the other hand, A has done little more than trot out a series of historical facts.

Thus, if you find yourself writing a background essay relating to historical or cultural developments, make sure you try to delve beneath the most obvious surface facts. A further paragraph taken from an essay describing the Surrealist movement should help you to understand clearly what is expected of you, if you are to score well on this section of the paper.

C   *Surrealism was a mainly artistic movement which grew out of Dadaism and flourished in the late 1920s and the 1930s. Central to any work by a surrealist artist, was the concept of the dream as a basis for creation.[1] The dream world became a colourful source of imaginative paintings, dominated by bizarre figures, set in impossible or topsy-turvy situations, where floppy clocks and other objects from the childhood world abounded.[2] The foremost painters of this genre were Salvador Dali, Delvaux, Miro and Magritte. As one might expect of artists creating a dream world which overturned the established order,[3] many of the main surrealists were anti-establishment and abhorred the fiercely competitive society[4] in which they lived.*

This is basically a sound beginning, despite the cliché-ed reference to floppy clocks and opens the way for discussion of the following points:

1   the theory of dreams in general and the specific importance of Freud and Jung.
2   the significance of childhood and its symbols to the Surrealist movement, i.e. the flight from the horrendous real world of 1914–18 and later the implications of the Great Depression.
3   the iconoclastic nature of the surrealists.
4   the ironic fact that some were a great commercial success, despite their abhorrence of much of society.

The person writing this essay will set herself well on the way to success, if she now proceeds to ask the following questions, which are a standard pattern to adopt, if the subject is concerned with a movement or a political/historical era:

1 Why did the phenomenon come about?
2 Were there parallels outside the main sphere of influence? (With our example essayist, the obvious parallel to examine would be German Expressionism.)
3 What caused its (inevitable) decline?
4 How, if at all, does it still affect our society?

CRUX QUESTIONS

Always try to answer whichever of the following questions are relevant to your topic:

1 Why did this event/phenomenon occur?
2 Why did this person come to prominence?
3 What are the (universal) implications for all of us?
4 Name any parallels in other countries or civilizations.
5 Why could the event/phenomenon (not) have occurred in your own country?
6 Why could the individual (not) have risen to prominence in your own country?
7 What lessons has the person/incident/movement/period taught us?

If you apply the above list to any Type 1 background question, it will automatically help your interpretation.

ASSIGNMENTS

1 Draw up a list of main points summarizing the achievements of any one or more of the following:

Impressionism, Post-Impressionism, Fauvism, Cubism, Debussy, César Franck, Saint-Saëns, Charles de Gaulle, Georges Pompidou.

2 Draw up an essay plan, listing the main points relating to any ONE of the following:

The Dreyfus Affair, the Vichy Government, Algérie française, the Fifth Republic, French Indo-China.

TYPE 2 QUESTIONS

Background questions on specific literary texts have their own advantages and disadvantages. On the credit side, all the material on which you need to draw is contained within the compass of the set-text you have studied.

Contrarily, this type of essay contains its own traps, since you are required to sift diligently among a mass of detail for items which are relevant to your socio-historical theme. Hence, the largest pitfall, about which we have already talked at length, looms large. With this type of essay, it can be especially difficult to avoid story-telling!

For many of these questions, there is an almost standard format, along the lines:

What picture does X text give the reader of life/social problems/society, at the time when the author was writing/in the ... era?

The word *picture* is the one to which you should pay special attention! *Picture* does not mean an interminable recounting of a scene or of events. Instead of looking for narrative sequences, concentrate on picking out informative details and on attempting a degree of interpretation. Ask yourself:

(a) *What do we learn about living conditions?* Is life easy/a struggle/calm/frenzied/depressing/rewarding/superficial/meaningful, etc.?

(b) *What is the social environment like?* Are we presented with a uniform group of people/a mixed environment/a milieu which is culturally barren/rich in characters/artistic/competitive/easy-going, etc.?

(c) *What is the prevailing atmosphere?* Is it progressive/repressive/energetic/inert/hopeful/pessimistic?

(d) *How do people behave?* Are they (in)considerate/responsible/mean/honourable/individualistic/cohesive/determined/apathetic?

(e) *What is the effect of recent events?* Is it stimulating/shattering/ruinous/debilitating/regressive/encouraging?

(f) *What were communications like?* Were they rudimentary/improving/newly mechanized/modern/advanced/non-existent?

(g) *How did people amuse themselves?* Independently/in groups/simply/sophisticatedly/decently/immorally/cruelly?

(h) *What did they wear and have in their homes?* Is there evidence of different needs and aspirations/were people prevented from achieving anything more than a basic level of provision/is there great emphasis on possessions?

(j) *How was the political situation?* Was it complex/quiescent/dramatic/a time of change/historically most significant?

(k) *Is there evidence of the effect of war?* Is the prevailing atmosphere anxious/fearful/one of relief? Is it a time of rebuilding/of major efforts to maintain the peace?

(l) *How did powerful individuals affect the environment?* Do real or fictionalized figures of power enter the story? If not, are any referred to in passing? What insights do they offer into the corridors of power?

(m) *What lessons can we learn from looking into this part of the past?* Do the times related in the work reflect an era that was more peaceful/calm/(un)just/aggressive/straightforward/stable?

If you apply the above list to any Type 2 question, it will help you to interpret automatically and to avoid story-telling. Use it to help you with the following practice exercises.

ASSIGNMENTS

Draw up essay plans for each of the following questions, relating it to one only of your set-books. You need list only the main points.

4 What picture does the text give the reader of contemporary social problems?
5 What impressions does the reader gain of contemporary society from the work?
6 How accurately does the work reflect the political times in which it was written?
7 In what ways does the society presented differ radically from our own?

12

Examination Revision and Techniques

REVISION

You will already have come across some suggestions to help you with your revision in Chapter 4. They and the hints below are all based on the premise that it is possible to prepare yourself reasonably fully for most questions on a text without reading the whole of the book again in the last weeks preceding your examination. Although it is a good idea in principle to read right through a work when revising, in reality you often just do not have the time.

Don't worry too much about this, since there is nothing like a shortage of time to concentrate the mind! If you have made good notes on a book (see pages 35–38), you will be able to read through it quite quickly, searching out the main details and spending more time on the more significant sections.

Always bear the exam in mind when you start studying a new text. Highlight significant passages by underlining, or by a line down the margin. Make marginal notes relating to themes and to character traits, etc. When you come across points of repetition or of contrast, reminding you of something which has occurred some pages back, make a reference in the margin of both pages.

Keep a *scrap-book* of newspaper and magazine items which have any relevance at all to the books you are studying. The cuttings may be critical reviews of a new book by or about one of your authors, a film notice dealing with a similar theme to that of one of your set texts, or a picture of life in France, confirming, or contrasting with, a point your author has made. The cutting may even be something as simple as a photo of a place associated with one of your authors.

What is the use of such a scrap-book, especially for exam revision?

Remember that literature essays give you the opportunity to show more than a suitably detailed knowledge and understanding of a text. If you can reveal, in addition to these essentials, some awareness of the author and of his or her life, this will give you credit in the form of marks. More important, you will have earned the credit, because you will have achieved something worthwhile. You will probably have discovered some of the wider implications of that author for yourself.

In the same way, French films which deal with themes similar to those treated in your set texts, will once again act as a point of reference or of comparison. A small amount of such comparison in your essays will telegraph to the examiner your ability to draw parallels with things outside the text, which is one indication of a literate and lively mind.

Your scrap-book will be particularly useful when you are revising before your exam, since you will have set it out in a bright and thematic way. Your mind will retain much of the basic information in it, since colourful detail is something onto which the memory can latch with ease. Additionally, a scrap-book becomes something very personal and items from it included in your exam answers will have several advantages. Firstly, they will tend to transmit an impression of your own, *personal* enthusiasm in a way in which statements like 'Alain Fournier is a great author because . . .' never can. Secondly, some of the information will be much more up to date than, say, the background notes contained in the particular edition of the text which you happen to be using. Thirdly, and perhaps most importantly, because the details have come from items which *you* have selected for your scrap-book, they will be different from the material written by your neighbour and may even be sufficiently individual for you to stand out from the thousands of other candidates sitting the exam around the country. It is this individuality which may eventually mark out your work as something special.

ADDITIONAL SOURCES OF SCRAP-BOOK MATERIALS

Remember that you are entitled to single photocopies of small extracts from published works, provided they are genuinely for personal study.

You might photocopy photographs and drawings from social-history books of the period, pages showing historical parallels with England, examples of work by contemporary artists, small sections from literary histories (such as the Bordas and Michelet series) and *occasional* comments by literary critics.

EXAM QUESTION PREPARATION

A favourite summer-time occupation is question-spotting! At some time or other, most of us will have been guilty of poring over lists of past questions to try to guess precisely which questions on a set author will come up.

This is a dangerous activity similar to Russian roulette and not just because you may swot up the wrong questions! Even if the right one does appear on the paper, you may still have actually done yourself a disservice by banking on it, since other, alternative questions may have been easier or more exploitable, had you kept an open approach.

You are being advised not to look for *banker questions*. What else can you do to give yourself a good start in the exam-room?

There are strategies you can follow which will allow you a wide spread of preparation, to the extent that any essay can be half-written in your mind *before* you start the exam (see pages 36–37).

Although you have been advised not to look for a single question, you can still be fairly certain of the types of question that may be asked. The basic essay types are:

1 Character studies
2 Themes and implications
3 Success or failure/strengths or weaknesses of the work
4 Implications for you
5 Style/characteristic features
6 General appeal
7 How the work fits into a pattern or literary movement
8 Structure of the work

Very understandably, you will be thinking, 'Eight basic types of essay! How can I prepare all those and still have a clear idea of part of my essay before I even enter the room?'

Read through the advice on pages 35–38 again. Even if you cannot, or are not prepared to learn gradually and systematically a series of quotations from each book, you can identify a mixture of 20–30 crucial passages in the text, to which you can refer specifically without giving the author's exact words.

Next, go back to the list of the basic types of essay. Now that you have a fresh picture in your mind of the more important passages within the work, go through each type from character study to structure and think out for yourself which individual touches, events, traits will be relevant to which type of question. Gradually, you will be able to practise this at any time without any books in front of you. As you become used to the list and to working with it, you will be able to rehearse almost any standard question which is likely to occur. When, finally, you are confronted with the exam situation, your confidence should be greater since you will have practised the themes that crop up. Equally importantly, because of this training, you will recognize more quickly than many candidates the implications of particular questions: which are more straightforward or difficult, which suit your particular attitude to the work, which are best avoided. You will weigh up the situation more quickly and will be much more likely to make the best choice for yourself, since you will not have restricted yourself by preparing and praying for the home banker.

ASSIGNMENTS

1 In each of your set-texts identify 30 crucial passages and/or quotations.
2 For each of your set-texts, note the passages relevant to each basic essay type.
3 If you are in the early or middle stages of your advanced French course, start a literature scrap-book now.

EXAM TECHNIQUE

As soon as you have your exam-paper in front of you:

(a) Read through the questions on *all* your authors, before starting to write.
(b) Decide which questions you are going to answer.

(c) Decide the order in which you will answer, starting with your strongest and ending with your weakest title.

(d) Write a brief plan for each essay before you start to write the essay proper.

(e) Apportion your time correctly, i.e. if the exam is three hours long and you have four questions to answer, try to allow ¾ hour for each, unless your last is sufficiently weak that part of its time is better given to the other three.

(f) Keep watching the time to make sure you follow your schedule. If there is not likely to be a central clock, make sure you take a watch to the exam room.

(g) Keep checking what you write against the title, to avoid digression.

(h) Include a reasonable amount of quotation in your answers, if at all possible.

(i) Make sure you give each essay a definite conclusion, so that it does not simply peter out.

ASSIGNMENTS

4 Obtain one of your examination board's past papers, decide before you look at it on which author you intend to write an answer, shut yourself away for the stipulated time, write an essay and hand it to your teacher/lecturer for comment. Do not look at any books while you are attempting this exercise.

5 Now do the same for a full past-paper, in one sitting.

EXAM ESSAY PLANS   (see also Chapter 6)

Because of pressure of time, you will not be in a position to draw up as detailed a plan as with a normal essay done in term or holiday time. The essentials to incorporate in your attenuated plan are:

(a) a one-line statement of each main point

(b) a list of items to be included in your introduction

(c) brief notes on your conclusion

(d) quotes to be included.

Below is an example of how such a plan might look. You will see that it does contain the important material, which is set out clearly enough to allow the candidate to write a logical smooth-flowing answer. Once again, do not fall into the trap of spending as long on your plan as on the writing of the actual essay.

Try to make sure that you produce a plan of some sort before you start the draft on which you are to be assessed. People who cannot be bothered to draw up an initial outline of their essay tend to end up writing a composition which *looks* as if they cannot be bothered. With a little planning, you will have made a good start towards producing something worthwhile.

ESSAY TITLE: <u>Discuss the significance of the theme of 'le couple parfait'</u>

<u>in Giraudoux's 'La Guerre de Troie n'aura pas lieu'</u>.

MAIN POINTS: 1 Inevitable slide into war almost retrieved by love (+

attendant qualities) Hector & Andromaque. Harmony v discord

Intro   Take up 'sonner faux'

2 Bitter irony of man's estate.

(Cassandre sets tone -)
                                                        Make ref.
'Il est aujourd'hui une chance pour que la paix s'installe to
                                                        'Sodome
sur le monde'. That chance Hec. & Andr.   et
                                                        Gomorrhe'

(Mutual understanding not intellectual, but intuitive -)

'On ne s'entend pas dans l'amour. La vie de deux époux

qui s'aiment, c'est une perte de sang-froid perpétuel'

(Despite Andr's words, high level of intuitive complicity -)

'Voilà . . . si Madame est ta femme, Madame peut être

fière.' Oiax, slapping Hector fails to comprehend their

empathy, man & woman in <u>harmony</u> (emphasize key-word)

(cf role of Hélène, Pâris' words -)

'Même au milieu de mes bras, Hélène est loin de moi.'

+ Hector's retort -

'Mais tu crois que cela vaut une guerre de permettre à

Paris de faire l'amour à la distance?'

('Harmonie intérieure' remains intact despite events -)

'Tu vois qu'il ne faut pas nous désespérer . . . De nous,

peut-être. Du monde, oui . . .' Peace crumbling round

them.

(Crushing irony of last two scenes -)

'le même battement de cils', etc.

'La guerre n'aura pas lieu.' - 'le poète troyen est mort.'

(Significance of 'le poète') for Hec. & Andr.

CONCLUSION: Take up point of last line, 'La parole est au poète grec.'

What has war to do with harmony and vice-versa?

13

Your Own Errors Of Style

If you are not happy with your essay style, there is a lot you can do to improve it quickly. The best way to start is to find a composition that you have already written, or, preferably, several such compositions, and to look for characteristic weaknesses in the ideas you have produced and the way you have expressed them. Most of your difficulties will be found in the list below.

BAD SPELLING

This particular blemish is mentioned first, partly because most of us are prone to it, and partly because it is a serious fault about which this book can do nothing, other than to point out the obvious. It is a blemish with which one can sympathize, because of the highly irregular nature of English spelling. Sympathy is not, however, enough, since for people writing literature essays, standards are high. It is unquestionably right that they should be so, as a glance at the two versions of the same paragraph below will confirm:

A   From almost the beginning of 'Les Dieux ont soif', we are aware that the legandary Greek figure of Orestes is an object of venaration for Évariste Gamelin. He admires his every dead, his every thought, his every caracteristic, so it is not serprising that the caracter of Évariste is influenced, subcontiously or otherwise by such hero-worrship.

B   From almost the beginning of 'Les Dieux ont soif', we are aware that the legendary Greek figure of Orestes is an object of veneration for Evariste Gamelin. He admires his every deed, his every thought, his every characteristic, so it is not surprising that the character of Evariste is influenced, subconsciously or otherwise, by such hero-worship.

The first version of the above paragraph was submitted by a student in his first year in the Sixth Form. The lesson is an obvious one for us, when we can recognize easily the spelling mistakes of others. We find it difficult to treat seriously what the essayist is saying, because the somewhat glaring errors intrude on our concentration and cause either irritation, or, as in the case of *dead*, possible mirth, which can be an even more damaging reaction than irritation.

If you yourself are not a good speller and do not make a determined effort to check the sort of words you know you get wrong, then you are likely to provoke the same sort of reaction in your readers as Paragraph A above.

This is a great pity. If we reflect on the correctly spelt version, we will see that the writer is making a perfectly valid point. He has clearly thought about his topic and has made a definite statement, which is worth the writing. It is a shame that his spelling undermines both his status and his credibility with us.

The moral is obvious. If you cannot spell, keep a dictionary by your side when you write. More important still, consult it whenever you are not sure of a spelling.

Turn to page 101 and complete Exercise A.

VAGUE OR IMPRECISE EXPRESSION

This is another difficult fault to correct, since it is not always easy to realize that you have committed it. One of the basic problems in writing a literature essay is the fact that you have to be far more precise than in ordinary conversation.

When you are talking to people, you can half-refer to things, leave sentences unfinished, rely on gestures, simply because your listeners will often be well aware of the situation about which you are talking and will only need to sift a few pieces of information from the words you use.

But when you are tackling an essay, beware of bringing your conversational habits to your literary style. Avoid writing unfinished ideas, partial analogies, incomplete references, careless syntax, as in:

> 'One can see that there is no lack of happiness, but it is the inability of the characters to accept it.'

ASSIGNMENT

Turn to page 102 and complete Exercise B.

LOOSE OR SLANG EXPRESSION

Again, this is a failing which you may have to make an effort to eradicate, since (a) it is so easy to fall into, (b) loose expression is often acceptable in conversation. The trouble is that, used in essays, it will irritate the reader and will stop you presenting your ideas accurately, since most colloquial expression is an approximation, e.g.

> One of Flaubert's great strengths as a writer was his determination to *do his own thing*.
> Fournier creates *tremendous* atmosphere in 'Le Grand Meaulnes.'
> The old outcast has the *living daylights* beaten out of him.

The items underlined in the examples above jar on the reader, and, more importantly, give less information than other choices of expression might have done.

ASSIGNMENT

Turn to page 102 and complete Exercise C.

CLICHÉ

Cliché is a close relation of loose expression. A cliché is a hackneyed expression which has lost its effectiveness and colour over the years through over-use. Phrases such as *carrying coals to Newcastle, black as night* are often quoted as examples. Such statements have almost no real meaning, since they trip so readily out of the brain and off the tongue that we do not think about them. They therefore indicate a lack of original thought. Think carefully when you are about to use one of these all-purpose formulae in a sentence and try to find an alternative in your own words.

ASSIGNMENT

Turn to page 103 and complete Exercise D.

INVOLVED WRITING

If, writing long sentences, in the course of which you employ many intricately linked subordinate clauses, the relationship between which is not always clear, and if, in so doing, you involve the reader in the tedious exercise of sifting through to determine exactly what is being said, you cause extreme irritation and, worse, fail to communicate to him the focus of your thoughts, then it would be hardly surprising if you were to alienate him from an essay, which, had it not been for the involved expression, might have contained much that was worth the saying.

The last sentence should have made the point clearly!

In general, sentences should be varied both in length and in the way you begin them. Try not to write too many which are more than four lines long. Also, you should avoid starting each one with the subject and verb. Here is an example of an involved sentence taken from an A-level essay

> The novel does lead us to the conclusion that happiness is unobtainable, perhaps in the sense that one cannot take possession of a state of mind such as happiness, or possibly in the sense that it is unwanted or that it is even unrecognized.

What did that sentence mean? Perhaps, but only perhaps, it may have been developing the following line of thought:

> 'The novel does lead us to the conclusion that happiness is unobtainable. Alain-Fournier seems to be saying that happiness is a state of mind. By its very nature, a state of mind cannot be possessed, since it is subject to frequent change. Additionally, there is the complication that happiness, when it is presented may not be wanted, or may even go unrecognized.

Whether or not the last paragraph is a correct interpretation is irrelevant. It is not the reader's job to sort out exactly what the writer means.

ASSIGNMENT

Turn to page 103 and complete Exercise E.

REPETITION

This is one of the commonest faults, for the reasons outlined elsewhere. Fortunately, it is also one of the easiest to eliminate. To establish the effect on the reader of excessive repetition, analyse your own reaction to the following paragraph:

> Perhaps the most striking quality of Verlaine's poetry is its musicality. He uses all the devices of poetry to produce this musical effect. Assonance and alliteration are used to great effect, as are all the different rhyming patterns and metres. Even within a single poem, he will vary the pattern of rhymes and metres, to achieve a whole variety of different effects.

Although the writer has clearly been unaware of repeating himself, you, the reader, will have noticed several examples and your mind, instead of following the flow of the ideas, will have stopped to make the wrong sort of observations. The mind searches for a little variety in what it reads.

If you have a tendency towards unnecessary repetition, you can start to help yourself immediately, by looking back through previous essays, paragraph by paragraph. Where you spot examples of this blemish, pencil in alternative expressions.

ASSIGNMENT

Turn to page 104 and complete Exercise F.

OVER-VERBALIZATION

Over-verbalization is a good name for this fault, since its very ugliness gives us a clue to its nature. It is the use of over-long, over-complex words and phrases to render situations which could have been expressed much more simply.

This sin usually occurs when people are trying to impress through the use of long words. It may be a result of over-exposure to zealous radio and television presenters, commentators and critics.

Whatever the reasons for it, if your prose contains a large number of long words, go back to the Anglo-Saxon!

The English language has two levels. Our basic survival vocabulary relating to everyday needs is Anglo-Saxon (e.g. eat, drink, sleep, awaken, bread, butter, flesh, blood), but our intellectual language, that of the courts, both legal and regal, is either Latin or French, which in itself is vulgar Latin (e.g. sentiment, discourse, entreaty, significance, sentence). If what we have written has ended up as something rather pompous or high-falutin', then, almost certainly, it will contain a high percentage of originally Latin vocabulary, e.g.:

> Thus a juxtaposition arises which invokes an element of emotional stupor, which is itself a causal factor in an ensuing, transient euphoria.

Even ten years after reading this statement in an essay, the present author is still not quite sure he knows what it means. Discussion with the original writer produced the following alternative:

Because the two events happen at the same time, they cause a shock to the system, which is enough to produce a temporary feeling of great happiness.

The alternative is much easier to understand, because it attempts to express a complex situation simply. The elements *juxtaposition, invokes, element of emotional stupor, causal factor, ensuing, transient euphoria,* have been substituted by *happen at the same time, shock to the system, temporary feeling of great happiness.*

This is not to say that words such as *juxtaposition, causal, transient, euphoria* have no place in the literary essay. Quite the opposite. Such language is totally appropriate, provided it is used sparingly. A large number of big words in one sentence will usually be too much for the brain to take. Besides, it will sound highly artificial.

ASSIGNMENT

Turn to page 104 and complete Exercise G.

PADDING

This blemish is endemic in most, if not all, essayists. For most of us, it remains below the surface, until we are called upon to write on a topic of which our knowledge is scanty or superficial. Then, we tend to fill out our paragraphs with irrelevant ideas and illustrations, and, most commonly, with woolly or background statements introduced at random to cover a lack of something to say.

Padding can be at least partly avoided with a little courage and by taking the following steps:

1 keep looking back at the title of your essay
2 avoid frequent use of long sentences
3 introduce relevant quotations
4 comment specifically on these
5 avoid overloading your essay with background information
6 avoid *guessing* at possible links between points
7 refrain from introducing side-issues.

EXERCISES

A SPELLING

Correct the spelling where necessary:

(a) Baudelaire underlines the correspondance between different sensations.
(b) There is in Malraux's novels something of an accomodation between his artistic and political perposes.
(c) Flaubert's achievements as a writer underline the creative author's need to practice his art.
(d) In a sense, both Meaulnes and François, preceeded by Frantz, persue an unatainable happiness.

(e) A minimum of vocablery is used, which is ingenously discriptive.

(f) Perturbed by this, she begins to doubt its relevance.

(g) The freinds percieve the preist's conciet.

(h) This development is only relitively succesfull.

(i) Albertine fullfills the requirements of her roll.

(j) The level on which they exist is scarcelly one of subsistance.

(k) This has become a definate obsesion.

B VAGUE EXPRESSION AND BAD SYNTAX

Tighten or correct each of the following:

(a) This is another example of Sartre's work which is difficult.

(b) The author examines the question of personal relations. He sees them at the bottom of our behaviour.

(c) Chamson is a modern author. He sees problems as they are.

(d) Baudelaire achieves a poetic whole.

(e) The two works are a pair.

(f) Pagnol's plays have a light style. They are easy.

(g) He lives alone with his mother in Paris, a tall, handsome schoolboy.

(h) With reference to his spiritual development, it is not surprising.

(i) Another quality of Fournier's that creates an element of mystery, is that of light.

(j) By writing 'une femme ou une jeune fille' retains this element of suspense.

(k) As a largely catholic population, the mother figure is something very sacred to them.

C POPULAR AND SLANG EXPRESSION

Rewrite these sentences in a more suitable style:

(a) One must watch out and not miss happiness, as those in the novel have done.

(b) This is much more realistic than a Cinderella-type ending.

(c) We are brought into the story with a bang.

(d) The father's irrational behaviour had a knock-on effect.

(e) The maid can't be doing with such behaviour from her master.

(f) You've got to agree with Vailland when he makes this point.

(g) The discovery absolutely fascinates him.

(h) He decides he will get one back on her.

(i) Again the irony of life smacks Marise across the face.

(j) She is aglow.

(k) The ending sticks out a mile.

(l) Gaston, who is not into social conversation, finds himself at a bit of a loss.

(m) Bazin's picture of the woman is certainly pretty horrendous.

(n) Looking after number one is the name of the game.

(o) The battle is really reaching a high by this stage.

D CLICHÉ

Re-write each of the following sentences, eliminating the clichés:

(a) During her absence, he describes himself as being like a fish out of water.
(b) He is a bewildered young boy, starved of affection.
(c) Money is seen to be the root of all evil in this play.
(d) By keeping them apart he manages to divide and conquer.
(e) When he murders his wife and blames it on Serge, he kills two birds with one stone.
(f) Isaïe is like a lost sheep without his brother, Marcellin.
(g) The author describes landscapes with a painter's eye.
(h) The novel ends on an optimistic note, with the suggestion that the three will live happily ever after.
(i) We always have the impression that Bernard is tied to her apron-strings.

E INVOLVED WRITING

Re-write the following so they may be understood. In each case, you may use several shorter sentences.

(a) This conception could easily be valid, since the fragmentation would never seem to present an idealistic picture without some form of pending turbulence or threatening event, the latter category being most obviously evident in the events which occur at the wedding-party.
(b) But perhaps it is one's definition of happiness which decides the answer, since, given the dream-like quality of the novel, happiness does appear to be illusory and it is clearly seen that not one of the principal characters obtains a lasting happiness, but surely this is much more realistic than a highly optimistic conclusion, where the couples depart enveloped in the roseate glow of the setting sun?
(c) To me they appear content with what they have up to a point, but are also aware of what they have missed, especially Xavier, who seems to note and understand the situation more than anyone, but is powerless to impose even in the case of Christian and Yveline's elopement, notwithstanding the efforts made, since his influence on them is not sufficiently great, or his gifts of persuasion up to the task.
(d) Whether or not the conclusion of the work may be said to be optimistic depends upon one thing, namely, assuming a degree of good will on the part of the author and some measure of integrity, whether the final events are to be seen as conclusive, assuming they have been accurately reported, or whether there is the implication that they are a further stage in a continuing process towards the light.

F REPETITION

Wherever possible, find alternatives for unnecessary repetitions:

(a) Maupassant uses as little description as possible in his stories. He uses description to provide the background to his stories.

(b) He considers alternatives, such as considering himself someone else's son.

(c) This thought concludes a certain line of thought.

(d) This power is a powerful quality, since this situation can alter as a consequence of this family's efforts.

(e) She perceives the problem and thinks the problem through. She then resolves to act. She takes it to its logical resolution.

(f) Definitely, we are left with a definitive statement.

(g) Supposing this to be true, I suppose we should accept the situation.

(h) This is the first time that we are presented with the author's theory of time.

(i) It is at this point that his real hate and his obsession with hate begin to develop to the point where the relationship between him and his mother reaches a new level of hatred.

G OVER-VERBALIZATION

Simplify the complex expression in the following:

(a) Utilizing a whole gamut of strategies, Voltaire achieves a style, which is the quintessence of the genre.

(b) The author functions as the disenfranchised observer of a society incohesive to the point of self-annihilation.

(c) The above statement retains a prototypal validity, redolent of perspicacious observation.

(d) Description contributes a crucial validity and verisimilitude to this fictionalized *compte rendu.*

(e) The author interpolates tangential comment to attenuate our response.

(f) The latent incongruity existing between the two siblings impinges upon the conscious recollection of the reader.

(g) Well may it be said to be the fulcrum of the action, maintaining plot and character in a constant, constructive balance.

(h) Dare one perceive a scintilla of optimism in this symbiotic relationship?

H GRAMMATICAL INACCURACY

Correct the grammar where required in the sentences below:

(a) It was her fate that she should be hung from a gibbet.

(b) Between he and she, there was a secret understanding.

(c) His inconsistency and lack of stability was the prime reason.

(d) This was a continual process, lasting intermittently for some twenty years.

(e) There was only the three of them who had a motive for the crime.

(f) No one were able to understand why he had written it.

(g) He had not been aware of the situation, never.

(h) Languishing in prison, she gave the convicted prisoner hope through her many visits.

(i) Many of Maupassant's *contes* were written for periodicals, a very demanding media.

(j) It was through the death of his grandmother, with who he had led a happy life.

(k) Albert's criticism of his father is becoming more sharper.

(l) He wont tell her what she wants to know.

(m) His secret resentment turns into defiancy.

(n) When the confrontation eventually came, she won her opponents with ease.

(o) The autopsy proved that she had drownded accidentally.

14

The French Cinema

Unless you are preparing for one of a very small minority of the Examination Boards, you may be surprised to encounter a chapter on the cinema in a book dealing with literature essay-writing. This is understandable, particularly if you have little or no experience of the French cinema. If, however, names like Jean Renoir, Godard, Truffaut, Chabrol and Lelouche already mean something to you, you will have some awareness of the link between literature and the film. It may also interest you to know that certain writers in the 1930s felt that the place of the novel, at least, would be taken over by what was then a new art form. This was the cinema.

Regrettably, it is still somewhat unusual for a French cinema topic to figure among the general questions on the literature paper, but this is no reason for ignoring what has become one of the creative high-points of twentieth-century French culture, especially when it can help you develop your feeling for literature.

At this point, you may be wondering how the printed page and 35 mm celluloid can have that much in common. If you pause for a moment to remember that one of the basic justifications for studying literature is the way it can help you increase your receptivity to people, your ability to share in their joys and predicaments, then the link between book and film becomes clearer. The commercial world has long recognized this relationship and has freely admitted as much by paying large sums of money to secure the film rights on a whole range of fictional material.

Although it is worth developing an interest in the French cinema for its own sake, let us be more pragmatic at this stage and think how seeing films can help you with your literature paper.

We have already discussed how literature increases the reader's sensitivity towards other people. It does this by placing its characters in specific situations, which we may view from the outside, even though the tension and inter-play may be such that catharsis occurs and we become personally involved on a temporary basis.

The cinema does this too, often with heightened effect. Thus, when we watch a fictional film, many of the skills of observation and analysis discussed in previous chapters come into play. We are practising, above all, the skills of interpretation and of participation in the fictionalized lives of others. By understanding more of other people, we come to understand our own natures better and may become more sensitive, more compassionate and more developed individuals. If the cinema contributes to this development, then any increase in such faculties will have a transfer effect when we come to read a book.

This is very fine, and to some extent highly altruistic, since few of us read a book or watch a film with the single-minded and conscious intention of becoming a better person. We do it, rather, for enjoyment. Instead of concentrating on the improvement of our inner selves, let us, then, examine what the French cinema can do practically to help you with your study of specific texts for a precisely defined examination.

FILM VERSIONS OF SET TEXTS

This is perhaps the most obvious way in which the cinema can help you with your course of study. There have been famous screen versions made of many of the great modern works, such as *La Bête humaine, Thérèse Desqueyroux, La Symphonie pastorale, Madame Bovary, Le Grand Meaulnes.*

Regional Arts Centres may run a film theatre, and many large and medium-sized towns will have a film club, which will show some French films. If your school is not already involved in any scheme for cinema visits, bring any opportunities you may spot in the press to the attention of your French teacher(s). Trips can easily be arranged, usually at reduced rates.

If you happen to live in a relatively isolated area where such visits are impracticable, you will find that occasionally among the fairly large number of French films screened on television, there will be one of your set works.

An important thing to remember is that, if you can show sufficient enthusiasm and generate enough support among other sixth-formers, students, parents and teachers, local clubs can be persuaded to put on a programme especially for you. If there is no club available, it is not difficult to start one, provided you have enough support.

Once you have got as far as actually seeing the desired film, you will find that the visual impressions will help you to make sense of items which may previously have escaped you, or the full implications of which you may not have caught.

THE DRAWING OF PARALLELS

Most of the films you will have the opportunity of seeing will not be directly related to your set texts, yet they will allow you to see points of comparison or of relation.

Imagine that you have just seen one of the most famous of all French films, *La grande illusion*, an eloquent and timeless plea for peace and international understanding. Some aspects of the First World War strike a modern viewer most forcibly – the sensitive camaraderie of brother officers, their code of honour and, contrastingly, the Colonel Blimp mentality of those who actually control the war.

If you have among your texts one of Malraux's war novels or the later stages of Sartre's *Les Chemins de la liberté*, then the film is bound to strike chords for you. You will notice differences in the way in which Jean Renoir, Malraux and

Sartre view comradeship. For both Malraux and Sartre, the individual is more isolated than Renoir's creations, with the interesting exception of the German commandant, von Rauffenstein.

Having noted the differences and the similarities, the common themes and the contrasts in attitudes, you will already understand more sharply the implications of what you have read. Similarly, the realization that different creative people do not have precisely the same attitudes to common themes leads you to an important discovery which you must make for yourself. No one artist, writer, film-maker has a monopoly on truthful observation. Human nature and the many millions of human beings who inhabit this planet are so complex that it is possible for both Jean Renoir and Malraux to be right when at times they appear to be taking up contradictory stances on the individual and his isolation.

As you grow used to watching films and looking for parallels, you will soon reach the position of putting some of your observations into your essays, e.g.

In *La grande illusion* Rosenthal, l'ingénieur, l'acteur and l'instituteur seem altogether more straightforward creations than the soldiers with whom Mathieu is surrounded. Is this merely the reflection of a simpler age, or of the fact that Sartre's characters think like Sartre himself?

THE DEVELOPMENT OF LANGUAGE SKILLS

If you have never seen and listened to a French film before, you may be a little disconcerted the first time because you find the speed of the language rather too fast for comfort. Do not be put off. After you have watched half a dozen films, you will find you can follow a great deal of what is said without having to rely on the sub-titles. In addition, you will have started acquiring a great deal of new language, which will, of course, help you with your reading of new texts.

A video-recorder or cassette tape-recorder can help you develop such skills, if you take the trouble to tape for your own private listening sections of the sound commentary of a film you have watched. You can replay short sections to learn the language and, once you have done this, you can listen through the passages and assess character and situations from the tone of voice and the accent used. Once again, you will be developing your interpretative faculties.

INCREASING YOUR BACKGROUND KNOWLEDGE

Films are often as important for the small and unexpected things which come out of them, as for the main themes and characters. For example, Chabrol's *Le Boucher* (see page 112) is a brilliant evocation not only of the hesitant, developing relationship between two isolated individuals and of its consequent destruction, but also of the quiet pleasures of French small country-town life. There are any amount of insights into the lives of ordinary folk – their eating habits, what happens at a wedding-breakfast, the importance to the community of the local school.

Once you have seen half a dozen or so French films, you will have a somewhat better idea of the myriad small details which make up life in France. Thus, when you read a book, your increased knowledge of the atmosphere and the environment will help you towards a greater feeling for the text. After all, a French writer, remember, writes principally for his or her own countrymen. Many of the smaller touches are bound to mean more to them than to a foreigner, who, for example, has no idea of French patterns of work, which are very different from the British, or of the communal significance of the evening meal in France. If we begin to understand these through what we see and hear on film, then our future understanding of literature will be the richer.

A GROWING INVOLVEMENT IN AND AFFECTION FOR FRANCE

The more French films you see, the more you will know and understand about the country. With knowledge, there usually comes an increase in affection. If you have not yet been to France for any length of time, seeing a few films will give you the beginnings of a familiarity with and a feeling for the country, itself. This should help you to tackle literature essay-writing with more enthusiasm, simply because you will know a little more about the background to your subject. Do not be afraid to communicate this enthusiasm when you write. Provided you do not fall into the trap of using exaggerated expression to communicate your pleasure, enthusiasm for your topic is usually infectious.

A MAJOR PITFALL

Unfortunately, it is all too easy to become blinded by the glamour of the medium. It is possible to see France as populated by a race of *Michèle Morgan, Anouk Aimée, Jean Gabin, Yves Montand, Jean-Paul Belmondo, Alain Delon, Isabelle Adjani,* living their lives on racing-car circuits, in colourful bars, first class train compartments or on film-sets. Try always to look for the real France behind the glamour of the scene.

HOW TO DEVELOP AN INTEREST IN THE FRENCH CINEMA

You have already been advised to start visiting appropriate film clubs or theatres and to watch the BBC's relatively large output of French films. Where the latter can prove particularly helpful to you is in their presentation of series and mini-series on major film-makers. The short season of Chabrol's films, for example, gives a fair representation of his work. If you keep the cuttings from the *Radio Times*, you will find them helpful, not simply to jog your memory as to the content of the film, but as guidelines to some of the points to note. The short notices do not usually tell you overmuch, but will often serve as a *point de départ* for determining your own reaction to the film.

Reading the notice on *La route de Corinthe*, for example, would have prepared you for making up your own mind whether the film was 'curious' and to what degree it was 'silly'. Again, with *Le Boucher*, you would have to make your own assessment of whether or not Stéphane Audran and Jean Yanne's performances were 'moving'.

You will also find it helpful to make short notes on a film soon after you have seen it. You might refer to the realism of the characters and of the background, the development of the plot, the maintenance of dramatic tension, etc. These notes could be kept with your film-cuttings in a scrap-book, much as suggested in Chapter 11. You will be surprised just how much detail from them can be related to your set texts.

TELEVISION DRAMA

Although not strictly speaking cinema, television drama provides many opportunities for viewing film versions of literary classics. *Germinal*, *Madame Bovary*, *Nana*, *Les Chemins de la liberté* and *Thérèse Raquin* have all been adapted for television during the past few years. Generally, they have been of an extremely high standard and eminently watchable. Although such productions are, of course, presented in English, they will allow you greater insights into the original texts. Additionally, producers' and reviewers' notes, as in the example on page 111 from *The Roads to Freedom*, will provide topical references and straightforward analysis to supplement the notes you already have on the books or authors.

ASSIGNMENTS

1 Basing your work on a film notice in the *Radio Times*, write your own notice of 100–150 words on a film you have seen, concentrating particularly on those points where you (dis)agree strongly with what the reviewer has said.

2 Write a review of 100 words on an imaginary film production of any of your set texts.

3 If you are in the early stages of your French course, start a cinema scrap-book now!

4 If you have seen a recent English-language production of a French work, write a commentary of 300 words on what you learnt from it of the author and his/her world.

5 Make notes on the background knowledge of France you have acquired from any French film you have seen recently.

6 Make notes on points of comparison and contrast between any French film(s) you have seen recently and one of your set texts.

WHAT DOES IT COST TO BECOME FREE?

France 1938–40 In his trilogy **The Roads to Freedom** Jean-Paul Sartre, the great French philosopher and political thinker, used the novel to explore one of the central problems of modern man: how to achieve personal and political freedom in a world of moral and social chaos. The three novels, *The Age of Reason, The Reprieve*, and *Iron in the Soul*, are set against the bleak background of France on the edge of the second world war, and he created a group of characters who stand out in modern fiction: self-questioning and fallible, they live out a tangled 20th-century morality play, struggling for love, friendship, and commitment as Europe heads towards disaster.

Their predicament, writes Anne Chisholm, was conditioned by political events that Sartre had just lived through, but their struggle is just as relevant today. The events are different, but the problem remains the same.

Unlike most novels that have translated successfully into television terms, *The Roads to Freedom* (Sunday 10.5 BBC2) is structurally as well as intellectually complex. In turning it into 13 parts, the BBC has probably attempted its most challenging serialisation yet.

As in the novels, the three parts remain clearly defined, and at the centre of them all is the character of Mathieu Delarue, the intellectual who thinks too much and asks too many questions to be able to commit himself to anyone or anything.

James Cellan Jones, the director, sees Mathieu and the two other main characters, Brunet, the committed Communist, and Daniel, the reluctant homosexual, as three alter egos for Sartre himself: 'but Mathieu is the one for whom he feels the most consistent sympathy.'

The only actor that James Cellan Jones could see in the part of Mathieu was, he says, Michael Bryant. Why? Bryant, a thoroughly professional self-aware actor, himself guardedly suggests an affinity to Mathieu.

'He's **in** me – he's one of the facets of me. One of the people I know he's inef-

fectual, yes, but cool with it. He's unbothered with life – no, capable of coping with life. I find coolness attractive.' Bryant's own life looks rather more satisfactory than Mathieu's with a beautiful wife, four children, and – his consuming passion – a boat. A slight, fair man, looking younger than 42, he dislikes talking about acting. 'Couldn't we talk about something sensible, like sailing or politics?'

He sees the current relevance of *The Roads to Freedom* theme. 'It's relevant to every generation, but it's especially applicable to young people. The cool thing – getting outside and looking objectively at yourself – is very much of today. That's why I like it.' Bryant is aware of the difference between Mathieu in the novels and Mathieu alive on the screen. 'I suppose I try to make Mathieu human and funny. He is rather the victim of circumstances over which he has little control. It's the actor's job to inject him with a kind of attractiveness, an individual beauty, which might not be what Sartre intended.'

Although Daniel, played by Daniel Massey, and Brunet, played by Donald Burton, are vital to the story, it is Mathieu who gives it coherence. David Turner the playwright who dramatised the novels sees Mathieu as 'the Hamlet of our age – Hamlet with a social conscience.'

9.15 pm
Chabrol—A Tribute to the Master:
Le Boucher

starring
Stéphane Audran, Jean Yanne
A short season of films by Claude Chabrol, a fervent admirer of Hitchcock, opens with the psychological thriller which many people consider his masterpiece.
After 15 years in the army, Popaul Thomas returns to Périgord to run his late father's butcher's shop. He meets the local schoolteacher, Hélène Marcoux, and an uncertain, platonic relationship begins. Then, in a nearby village, a young girl is found stabbed to death.

Hélène Marcoux	STÉPHANE AUDRAN
Popaul Thomas	JEAN YANNE
Angelo	ANTONIO PASSALIA
Léon Hamel	MARIO BECCARIA
Father Charpy	PASQUALE FERONE
Police Inspector	ROGER RUDEL
Charles	WILLIAM GUÉRAULT

Written and directed by
CLAUDE CHABROL
(*A French film with English subtitles*). *Films: page* 11
(*Next Saturday:*
La route de corinthe)

Le Boucher
1969 (9.15–10.45 BBC2 Colour) Claude Chabrol's magnificent movie, with Hitchcockian murder and guilt poking through placid village rituals; filmed on location with the same affection that flourished in his recent study of Breton peasants, *The Proud Ones*. Moving central performances from the director's wife, Stéphane Audran, and Jean Yanne.

9.10 pm
Chabrol—A Tribute to the Master:
The Road to Corinth

(*La Route de Corinthe*)
starring
Jean Seberg, Maurice Ronet
When a NATO security officer is shot dead in Greece, his wife, Shanny, is framed and convicted of his murder. Given three days to leave the country, she is determined to find her husband's killer first—in spite of active hindrance by NATO officials.
Chabrol's tongue-on-cheek espionage adventure makes stunning use of the Greek locations and includes many references to Hitchcock, the director he so admired.

Shanny	JEAN SEBERG
Dex	MAURICE RONET
Robert Ford	CHRISTIAN MARQUAND
Sharps	MICHEL BOUQUET
Skolikides	SARO URZI
Killer	ANTONIO PASSALIA
Josio	PAULO JUSTI
Alcibiades	CLAUDE CHABROL

Screenplay by
CLAUDE BRÛLÉ and DANIEL BOULANGER
Based on the novel *Fleuve Noir*
by CLAUDE RANK
Produced by ANDRÉ GÉNOVÈS
Directed by CLAUDE CHABROL
(*A French film with English subtitles*)
(*First showing on British television*)
Films: page 15

The Road to Corinth
1967 (9.10–10.50 BBC2 Colour) Curious relic from director Claude Chabrol's silly period. A flimsy spy yarn with Greek locations, fetching photography and much bizarre detail. Shown cut and dubbed in British cinemas, but this is the original version.

9.15 pm
Chabrol—A Tribute to the Master:
La femme infidèle

starring **Stéphane Audran**
Michel Bouquet
Michel Duchaussoy

Charles, a prosperous insurance broker with a beautiful wife, is well pleased with his life. Its impeccably ordered routine is for him the essence of happiness and success. So it comes as something of a shock when he realises that his wife is stepping out of the pattern and into a secret life of her own.

Claude Chabrol's minutely observed pictures of the French bourgeoisie, balancing ritual against passion, makes domestic murder a totally credible and comprehensible act.

Hélène Desvallées	STÉPHANE AUDRAN
Charles Desvallées	MICHEL BOUQUET
Victor Pegala	MAURICE RONET
Bignon	SERGE BENTO
Police Officer Duval	MICHEL DUCHAUSSOY
Police Officer Gobet	GUY MARLY
Michel	STÉPHANE DI NAPOLI
Maid	LOUISE CHEVALIER
Mother-in-law	LOUISE RIOTON
Paul	HENRI MARTEAU

Written and directed by CLAUDE CHABROL
A French film with English subtitles
Films: page 11

La femme infidèle

1968 (9.15–10.50 BBC2 Colour) Claude Chabrol at his most stunning: a story of murder among the French bourgeoisie in which all the director's tricks (meal scenes, jibes at TV, Hitchcock homages) slot into place and the characters are treated with loving care. Terrific acting, too, from Michel Bouquet and Stéphane Audran.

15

The Press

Newspaper and magazine articles are a valuable means of supplementing the information available in text-books. Not only do they give extra detail on a particular topic, they also provide insights which, by the very nature of the medium, tend to be much more up to date than a text-book can hope to be.

Often, new correspondence from or about a particular author will come to light, when, for example, a person of special significance has recently died, with the result that his or her story can now be told. The new information presented will sometimes explain moments of difficulty in relationships, or examples of enigmatic behaviour, which had hitherto been left open to interpretation.

So, for these reasons alone, it is a good policy as has been previously recommended, to keep a scrap-book of press-cuttings on relevant authors and personalities. But there are other equally important justifications.

NEWSPAPERS

Read through the reviews by Ms Tennant and Ms Tindall on pages 116 and 118 and you will become aware of a difference in approach from that used in books of criticism or in the standard, useful introductions to your set texts.

Emma Tennant and Gillian Tindall are not writing principally as learned academics, but as journalist-reviewers, whose task is to capture flavour, to convey briefly a sense of period and of the human qualities of Colette and Simone de Beauvoir. Additionally, both convey in their different ways their affection for their respective authors.

With Ms Tennant, commenting on a biography of Colette, the strength of feeling for her subject comes through in a most warming manner. Colette is, indeed, an author and a woman to admire and Ms Tennant succeeds in transmitting her admiration for her. Consequently, her own style is often emotive, even impassioned, but her purpose is not to write a work of scholarly calm. She is there to put her readers in the picture and, in this case, to convey her own enthusiasm and succeeds in communicating most strongly to us the essence both of Colette and of the biography in question. For those of you studying Colette, Ms Tennant has provided glimpses of the real person, which it is unlikely that you had previously caught.

After a relatively short review such as this, you will understand Colette better and your feeling for her is likely to have increased.

Ms Tindall's review of *Five Early Tales* by Simone de Beauvoir is in a contrasting style, since what is required here is in fact a form of literary criticism.

Yet we are still granted a series of insights, which are fascinating and which bring out the personal side of de Beauvoir.

The reference to Camus is absorbing and will be of practical interest to those of you studying his work. It also illustrates an important point:

DRAWING PARALLELS

We see from Ms Tindall's review that an article does not need to centre on one of your set authors for it to be of interest and of use. Something written about a writer of whom you have little or no knowledge will often contain an insightful reference to one of your own.

The way Ms Tindall has worked in the reference to Camus is also of use to you, as you develop your own literary style. Much has already been said about drawing parallels and finding points of contact between authors. Note how Ms Tindall employs this technique to establish a most useful *point de départ* for her review.

But, more importantly, articles such as these help to present the whole picture of a period, which the isolated study of 4–5 texts can rarely do. Furthermore, someone with a feeling for literature will be able to draw parallels between works, to trace common themes, to highlight contrasting attitudes and styles. Sensible reference to an author outside your set books can only help you.

For example, let us remain with Colette for a moment and assume that Proust is one of the authors whom you are studying. It would be relatively easy and wholly pertinent for you to comment on the contrasting styles and attitudes of two authors, much of whose work reflects aspects of the same society. A reference such as the one that follows, would show evidence of some understanding of the period.

> It is ironic that many readers should retain a distorted view of both authors' writings on the *Belle Époque*. To see in Proust and Colette nothing but a portrayal of male and female inversion in the characters of this period, is to undervalue seriously the picture they portray of a glittering society in general decay.
>
> As Ms. Emma Tennant recently pointed out in a *Sunday Times* review, higher standards should be expected 'when writing about the life of a woman as intelligent and sensual, as capable of writing of freedom and imprisonment, ... of maternal love and innocence, as Colette'.
>
> Much the same may be said for Proust.

SOURCES

A high proportion of the national press does not provide many literary articles or reviews, especially about non-English-language authors. The papers to which you have family access may fall into this category. Useful material will frequently be found in the following periodicals:

> *The Times; Financial Times; Guardian; Observer; Sunday Telegraph; Sunday Times; Times Educational Supplement; Times Literary Supplement; Radio Times; Listener; New Statesman; Punch; Spectator.*

The transformations of Colette

COLETTE was born Gabrielle ("Gabri") Colette in 1873 and she died plain Colette in 1954. In her eighty years she fell first from the cocoon as *ingénue*, wife of the philandering Monsieur Willy – and he could perhaps be described as a penpusher too, for his cruel gift was to push others to labour long hours with the pen and to recover the fruits for himself – and she fell again, after some years of freedom, to another *Barbe Bleu*, the Baron de Jouvenel. Colette's life was a series of transformations from chrysalis to butterfly and back again; the wonder is that she was able to spin herself back into safety so many times; to show herself, on the boards and on the page, with an extraordinary, seductive honesty, to collect enemies and friends at speed and to vanish back into herself again, to memories of childhood and Sido, the incomparable mother.

A weaker young woman, coming from a dowryless, bankrupted family in the provinces to marry M. Willy the remorseless exploiter, the gossip, the *bon viveur*, would have sunk into illness and insanity at this rough change of fortune. The country Colette loved was replaced by a dark, airless Paris room (and here she was locked every day to write the adventures of Claudine, M. Willy's latest invention); the mother who gave everything must now stand second to a monster of infidelity. In fact, Colette suffered for many years from a jealousy which made her, like a caged animal, capable of concentrating only on her master.

The life M. Willy led her made her droop with fatigue; the late rush to the offices of L'Echo de Paris, the hours of drinking at the Napolitain, Weber's, Pousset, followed by a day of forced writing. Worst of all was M. Willy's absolute power over what she wrote as well as over her person, to the extent of adding sentiments and sentences Colette would have been incapable of expressing. So that she must have known that unless she set herself free from him, the books she had written would never be completely hers.

Colette freed herself, away from the society and the gossip and into the world

COLETTE: A BIOGRAPHY by Michèle Sarde translated by Richard Miller/ Michael Joseph £12.95 pp 426

Emma Tennant

she later described in "La Vagabonde," the company of starving music-hall *artistes*, the tours with trunks densely packed with make-up and costumes, the intoxicating sense of being always on the move. And her lover now was the aristocratic Missy, the Marquise de Belbeuf, who mounted her own spectaculars, starred in them with her new *amie* and gave kindness and protection after the difficulties of leaving M. Willy. Her men's clothes and cropped hair led the irrepressible M. Willy to travel in the Women Only coach on trains and, when accosted, to protest: "But I'm the Marquise de Belbeuf!"

Sapphism was fashionable in those last years of the Belle Epoque. In describing these women – like Natalie Clifford Barney, a rich American and poetess who lived in the Rue Jacob, with its famous garden and *Temple de L'Amitié* – and in showing Colette's fascination too with the *Grandes Horizontales*, Liane de Pougy and La Belle Otéro, this biography gives plentiful and interesting detail. But, for all the attention paid to Colette's every stage in life – childhood and mushroom-picking with Sido, the marriage with M. Willy, the second marriage (and continual journalism, which like the Claudine labour seemed fated to go with the conjugal state: Henri de Jouvenel was editor of Le Matin); and then Goudeket, final husband, friend and companion – for all this, Michèle Sarde has not given us Colette.

We are given practically everything else. Ms Sarde's reflections on the position of women (which was pretty well always *horizontale* in those days) are tedious in the extreme – not because the subject is not of relevance, which it is, but because they, and other ponderous thoughts on motherhood, captivity, love and enslavement, go undigested with the stuff of Colette's life. It is strange that so little has been written about Colette, and disappointing to find the strained visions of Ms Sarde. Her rolling, emotive French has made a bad crossing into a sort of Frankee, rather than Franglais, and we have to suffer: "In her spotless shop, she was the fairy godmother in a white smock, in her laboratory, surrounded by her equipment. She also had a branch in Saint Tropez," as well as "Her last books reveal the shrinkage of her field of vision ..." and so on on every page. Tumbler-Dryer English will not do when writing about the life of a woman as intelligent and sensual, as capable of writing of freedom and imprisonment, Léa and Chéri, maternal love and innocence, as Colette.

If you do not have easy access to any of these sources, ask any friends and neighbours who take them to let you have their copies. The school library will have some of the list available and the local lending library will have all or most of them.

Current photocopying law allows you to take one copy of an article for personal use and most libraries now have a machine available for the purpose. Unfortunately, this costs money, but if an article is of reasonable interest, not even particularly important, your Modern Languages Department will surely make a copy, once you draw their attention to it.

If you find an article or a review particularly stimulating, do not be afraid to write to its author, who will usually be delighted that you have bothered to show your interest. This will not infrequently give you other material.

ASSIGNMENTS

1 Look patiently for several weeks until you find 3 or 4 newspaper articles or reviews relevant to French literature. Underline in each of them any points of interest which relate to your set authors. Show them to your teacher and ask her/his views.
2 Keep a scrap-book of such cuttings for a whole year and try to draw on it each time you have a literature essay to write.
3 If your school subscribes to *Paris Match*, *Le Point*, *L'Express* and/or *Le Nouvel Observateur*, scour through these for relevant cuttings, sharing the task with the other members of the Sixth Form studying Modern Languages.
4 If your school has an Assistant(e) or some other francophone person with extensive contacts in France, ask him/her to find other sources of articles and reviews for you.

Escaping the octopus

WHEN THINGS OF THE SPIRIT
COME FIRST: FIVE EARLY TALES
by Simone de Beauvoir/Deutsch and
Weidenfeld £6.95 pp 224

Gillian Tindall

"I know from my own experience", wrote Camus, 'that a man's life-work is nothing but a long journey to find again, by all the detours of art, the two or three powerful images on which his whole being opened for the first time.' Many writers would endorse this; Simone de Beauvoir surely would. (Camus was an associate of hers in the 1940s and appears, barely veiled, in *"Les Mandarins"*.)

She, more markedly than most novelists, recapitulates the same themes and even events in several different works; and, because she has also written extensive autobiography, she displays more readily than most the complex links between this fiction and the core of lived experience. Indeed the transformation of life into fiction, and the meaning that certain experiences have had for her in terms of her work, is in itself one of her key themes. The sources of psychic energy located in youth, and the failure of those sources with the going-on of time, has been one of her personal "two or three powerful images". Age and mutability are emotion-laden topics for most of us, but for de Beauvoir they seem almost intolerably significant: the key that has unlocked the door of life eventually reveals not-all-that-much lying behind it.

It is therefore something of a relief (and perhaps de Beauvoir has found it so herself) to turn from her more recent works, with their insidious but insistent theme of decline and betrayal, back to her youth where the images began. These five interlocked stories, each named after a different central female figure, which she wrote around the age of thirty, hold little that is surprising or even new for readers of her subsequent books, but they show the early stages of the writer's journey in a limpid and arresting light. Here, as "Anne", is Zaza, the family-hounded girl whose actual death is the key event of *"Mémoires d'une Jeune Fille Rangée"* ("and

it seemed to me for many years that I had paid for my own liberty with her death").

Here too, as "Marguerite" is the young de Beauvoir herself, wandering Montparnasse by night and getting into conversation with strange men, not from wantonness but from an innocent avidity for life on almost any terms rather than the death-in-the-family that Anne-Zaza suffered. And here, in "Chantal" we have, one suspects, another version of the author, posing and day-dreaming in a provincial lycée, for Simone de Beauvoir's capacity for romantic projection has always been marked, perhaps to a greater extent than she herself would allow. She also, to a non-French reader, has seemed consistently throughout her work more enmeshed in a specifically French society and way of thought than she appears to believe.

The title of this book (in French *"Quand Prime le Spirituel"*) is of course ironic. The theme that runs through each story is that things of the spirit do *not* necessarily come first, and that to discount the demands of the emotions and body is to court disaster in one form or another. But one must make the perhaps obvious comment that only someone reared in a particular kind of religion-imbued society does in fact imagine that things of the spirit come first. What this book shows is not so much the young learning what life is like, as the young painfully unlearning a blueprint for life which has initially set them on the wrong track. What we have here is not just human perception versus Catholic teaching, as in the books of our own but curiously un-English Antonia White: it is human nature struggling with the vast, soft, tough octopus of Catholicism institutionalised and secularised into the bourgeois ethic of a whole race. When de Beauvoir was born in 1908, and still when she grew to womanhood, that octopus flourished as never before and gripped almost every social level in France. To peel off its tentacles and escape (as she did) was not even so much a bid for freedom as the deliberate adoption of an opposing stance – "free thinking", left wing, anti-clerical – that in its own way was often as rigid as the one the octopus enjoined. Significantly, Marguerite, in what de Beauvoir rightly recognises as the best story in the book, escapes from the octopus by initially making her degenerate brother-in-law into an anti-saint and seeing the garish boulevards of Paris by night as if in an apocalyptic vision. Real emancipation only comes for her when "suddenly, instead of symbolic scenery, I saw around me a host of objects that seemed to exist in their own right".

The shifting viewpoint also operates as a sophisticated literary device: not only is the main character of each story a subsi-diary character in others, but the way in which each is presented differs subtly from story to story. It is as if the inexperienced author were already prepared (following Sartre) to confront that most intractable of literary problems – the validity of the ghostly narrator that runs the machine. "This book," she says, "is a beginner's piece of work." Yes, but it is not inconsiderable, not by any means quaint juvenilia. I am glad she decided to exhume it.

Sample Essays

[Written under open, non-examination conditions]
Essay 1 was produced by a student at the end of the First Year of an Advanced
Level Course and reflects the standard expected from a sound candidate at this
stage.
Essay 2 represents what may be reasonably expected of a competent student at
the end of an Advanced Level Course or even part way through a course of
further study.

ESSAY 1

*From your reading of Bazin's 'Vipère au poing', show how Jean's innocent attitude
slowly changes into seething hatred towards his mother.*

The conflict between mother and son in *Vipère au poing* may be divided into three
distinct stages. Jean is first made aware of his mother's failings through her
blatant cruelty towards her sons. The second phase to be noted is Jean's developing realization of his feelings for Mme. Rezeau coupled with his first attempts at
retaliation. The third stage is inevitably the culmination of these two, when Jean
is aware of his desire to take what he regards as a life for a life, since he regards
his mother as responsible for the death of his grandmother, with whom he was
so happy. The warning signs are early visible, when Mme. Rezeau's homecoming
proves that life is not going to be easy for the boys. As Jean says:

> Le nombre de kilogram-mètres dépensés par ces extrémités en direction de mes joues
> et mes fesses pose un intéressant problème de gaspillage et d'énergie.'

Clearly, the mother never has any reasonable quarrels to pick with the boys.
In fact, her utter pettiness forces her to deny them the things they enjoy:

> Le premier droit qui nous fut retiré fut celui de l'ourson ... ou petit tour.'

It is also evident throughout the book that she favours her youngest son,
Marcel, nicknamed 'Cropette' by Freddie and Jean. Such favouritism appears
to be an attempt on her part to divide the boys, so as to make it easier for her to
control them:

> 'Alors madame mère, condescendante, lui offrit le croûton qu'il préférait.'

What makes the favouritism seem worse, is the fact that Mme. Rezeau is
placing restrictions on Freddie and Jean and maintaining a check on what they
keep:

'Quelques jours après, rafle générale dans nos chambres et dans nos poches. Interdiction de conserver plus de quatre francs.'

As the book proceeds it is easy to perceive that Jean's criticism of his mother is becoming stronger and more fervent all the while. One of the major turning points must be when the boys are threatened with Borstal after being accused of poisoning the horses. In her own words, Mme. Rezeau wanted to

'condamner les coupables à la maison de correction.'

It is here that Jean's real hatred towards his mother begins to become an obsession. As yet, his feelings have been very much covert, as if he can only just begin to admit them:

'Si tu savais comme je ne t'aime pas!'

Although consciously unaware of the depth of his emotions, Jean now reveals in some of his apparently more casual utterances, how he sees the problem of his mother. The simple statement, 'Vengeance à Folcoche' suggests that his hatred for his mother is now becoming so strong, that her death may be the only way to end it.

Eventually, his secret hate for the woman turns into defiance. He will not tell her what she wants to know:

'Pour cet office-là ma mère, répondis-je calmement, vous avez Cropette.'

The irony of this comment is self-evident. Mme. Rezeau has spoilt Cropette, let him fulfil her needs. It is at this juncture that the mother realizes that she sees herself in her son:

'Cette attitude ne sembla pas déplaire à Folcoche, qui eût fait un excellent officier de corps francs. Un mélange d'inquiétude et de considération se lisait sur son visage.'

At this point one notices a change in her attitude. She no longer wishes to be separated from the boys. Jean has challenged her:

'L'idée de s'absenter pour deux mois l'épouvantait: que resterait-il de son empire lors de son retour . . . ? Et notre mère changeant d'avis regardait avec inquiétude monter nos épaules.'

Already Jean is obtaining genuine satisfaction from his strongly negative relationship with his mother:

'Je fus étonné de l'expression de son visage. Les traits de Folcoche, dans le sommeil, s'amollissaient. Le menton lui-même perdait de sa sécheresse. Oui la vipère, tous yeux éteints, la vipère, du pied du platane, une fois morte, manquait de métal.'

This is a considerable contrast with the viper at the beginning of the novel. The wanton cruelty is gone.

By the time Mme. Rezeau is taken into hospital, Jean's feelings for her are such that to wave to her is too much:

'Au commandement nos mouchoirs furent agités.'

Throughout the mother's stay in hospital and her near-fatal illness, the question is raised as to whether it is actually her own hatred which has pulled her through:

'Évidemment Folcoche ne mourut point. Elle fut seulement réopérée.'

The clinical nature of this comment seems to reflect the hardness of her son's own attitude. And it is now that the conflict between mother and son moves towards its climax. For Jean, it is no longer simply a question of subconscious or covert hatred and occasional comment. The strength of his feelings leads to a contest of wills:

'Non, Folcoche, tu ne parviendras pas à empoisonner notre joie.'

The situation is complicated by the fact that Jean like Mme. Rezeau feels a need for the conflict to continue. Whilst she is away, he describes himself almost as the proverbial fish out of water:

'Personne pour nous surveiller. Ce laisser-aller n'était-il pas un piège tendu à notre discrétion?'

The need for battle deepens and becomes yet more serious in its implications, since the relationship with his mother has become almost a raison d'être:

'Effectivement. Jouer avec le feu, manier délicatement la vipère, n'était-ce point depuis longtemps ma joie favorite? Folcoche m'était devenue indispensable comme la rente du mutilé qui vit sa blessure.'

When Mme. Rezeau returns the next time she begins once more to disrupt the unity of her sons. The difference now is that her primary motivation is to attack Jean. Thus, she punishes Freddie for one of Jean's actions simply to promote bad feeling between the boys:

'J'ai trouvé aussi des clefs qu'*il* destinait certainement à mes serrures.'

In the final stages of Jean's hatred, the preceding factors coalesce and, worse, what were formerly abstract notions have taken concrete form in Jean's mind. He is now certain that he is fighting a war with his mother:

'La guerre civile continua.'

He sees his mother in the viper he first killed:

'Je saisis la vipère par le cou, exactement au-dessus de la tête, et je serrai, voilà tout.'

His decision to kill the mother-kingfisher proves symbolical of his hatred of his own mother:

'On n'étouffe que les serpents, ou les pigeonneaux ou encore les perdrix blessées. Je choisis une épingle parmi celles qui se trouvaient piquées sous le revers de mon veston et lentement, je l'enfonçai sous l'aile de l'oiseau.'

Inevitably, Jean's hatred does not stop at birds and vipers any longer. These killings merely cover the fact that he now needs to kill his mother:

'Je donnai un brusque coup de barre à droite. Folcoche tomba dans la rivière.'

Unfortunately for the boys, Folcoche does not drown, just as she did not die when they tried to poison her. Ironic as it may seem, it is perhaps as well for Jean that she does not die, since it is evident at the end of the work that Jean's principal reason for living is the angry, violent passion he feels against his mother. Mme. Rezeau is apparently indestructible, as are Jean's feelings towards her. When eventually the mother dies, of one thing we may be certain: the person dies, but the relationship lives on.

'Cette vipère, ta vipère, je la brandis, je la secoue, je m'avance dans la vie avec ce trophée, effarouchant mon public, faisant le vide autour de moi. Merci, ma mère! Je suis celui qui marche, une vipère au poing.'

ESSAY 2

The Theme of Violence in Maupassant's Work

Throughout his large output of contes, nouvelles and novels, Maupassant returns time and again to the theme of man's inherent violence. Contes such as *Un Bandit corse, Le Gueux, La Mère Sauvage* and *Pierrot* all present insights into this facet of the human animal and reveal the writer's skill as an observer of behaviour. Yet Maupassant does not simply take instances of overtly violent behaviour and tell the reader to look how aggressive our species is. Instead, he reveals the many-sidedness of what is apparently a simple phenomenon. In *Un Bandit corse*, for example, Sainte-Lucie only acts violently after a quiescent youth and considerable recent provocation, but, when it occurs, the reaction is extreme:

'regardant en face le meurtrier, il cria: "C'est le moment!" puis, à bout portant, il lui creva la poitrine.'

But it is not Maupassant's purpose simply to portray the act of violence. What interests him and what he communicates to the reader is the underlying condition which brings about the aggression. Thus, *Un Bandit corse* becomes a carefully structured tale in which the harshness of the physical and, indeed, the emotional environment of the Corsicans is seen to produce harsh adults.

The searing heat and the asperities of the landscape impress upon the reader the unrelenting harshness of the land and the climate:

'Nous hâtions le pas pour atteindre avant la nuit le petit village d'Albertacce, sorte de tas de pierres soudées aux flancs de pierre de la gorge sauvage.'

Even the village of Albertacce, in which Maupassant and his companion seek refuge for the night, is itself taking shelter from the elements.

Once a calculated insult on the part of his father's killer has triggered-off Sainte-Lucie's vengeance, he reacts instinctively and the economy of Maupassant's style reflects the economy of thought behind the young bandit's actions. Thus, when Sainte-Lucie has to take the decision whether or not to kill one of his wounded adversaries, he approaches the matter as if the man were a badly wounded animal:

'Il considéra la plaie, la jugea mortelle, rechargea lentement son fusil, invita le blessé à faire une prière, puis il lui brisa le crâne.'

The story concludes with a comment by a local man who has retold the events:

'Que voulez-vous? on fait son devoir.'

One does one's duty. One is what one is. The Corsican is conditioned by his surroundings. He is seen by Maupassant to be a product of his own immediate environment, part of a dispassionate and amoral natural process.

In *La Mère Sauvage*, Maupassant takes up one of his favourite themes, the Franco-Prussian War of 1871, to continue his analysis of the types of violence which lead to death. Sauvage, who runs a small farm, has had four young Prussian soldiers billeted on her during the occupation. She and they develop a tolerable and, at times, almost agreeable *modus vivendi*, but this is broken by news of the death of her only son, Victor, at the Front. When the young soldiers are burnt to death by Sauvage as a gruesome revenge, she faces the firing squad unrepentantly at the end of the tale.

These are the bare bones of a narrative which might have been a simple story of violent action, but Maupassant's purpose is more complex. Although the four youths are described as physical stereotypes – blond, blue-eyed, well-built –

'quatre gros garçons à la chair blonde, à la barbe blonde, aux yeux bleus, demeurés gras malgré les fatigues qu'ils avaient endurées déjà' –

they are shown to be good-hearted boys, who display kindness and consideration towards Sauvage:

'Seuls chez cette femme âgée, ils se montrèrent pleins de prévenances pour elle, lui épargnant, autant qu'ils le pouvaient, des fatigues et des dépenses.'

Consequently, when they are eventually burned to death, the reader is already conditioned to see the irony of the situation and to feel much compassion for the victims. Even the Prussian officer in charge of the investigation and the clearing-up operation is given impeccable credentials, so that any germanophobia on the part of the reader is suppressed. He is:

'un officier allemand qui parlait le français comme un fils de France.'

Maupassant's point is a clear one. The young soldiers are not themselves to blame for what is to happen to them. Violence lies inside of the individual who produces it and is often a result of deep passions over which there is little control:

'La vieille Sauvage restait debout, devant son logis détruit, armée de son fusil, celui du fils, de crainte qu'un des hommes n'échappât.'

Even when one might have expected the old woman's passion to be exorcised by the act of setting her own dwelling on fire, her compulsion is still strong enough for her to stay resolutely on guard, determined that her revenge shall be total. For Sauvage, it is sufficient that the Prussian army in general is responsible for the death of Victor. Individual Prussians, no matter how good they have been to her, are equally culpable. This is exemplified in the orderly way in which she ties up the loose ends of the execution by fire:

'Quand elle eut fini, elle tira de sa poche deux papiers, et, pour les distinguer aux dernières lueurs du feu, elle ajusta encore ses lunettes, puis elle prononça, montrant l'un: "Ça, c'est la mort de Victor." Montrant l'autre, elle ajouta, en désignant les ruines rouges d'un coup de tête: "Ça, c'est leurs noms pour qu'on écrive chez eux." '

Her action has not been simply impulsive, but has been worked out, step by step – hence, her final composure:

'douze hommes se rangèrent vivement en face d'elle, à vingt mètres. Elle ne bougea point. Elle avait compris; elle attendait.

Unlike Sainte-Lucie's initial killing, the murder Sauvage carries out is not of the individuals directly responsible for Victor's death, but it involves those who are at best guilty by implication and bear a form of corporate responsibility. In a sense, the young Germans fall victim to Sauvage's need to inflict compensatory violence on someone who may assume symbolical guilt. This underlying point is finally borne out by the way she accepts her fate with equanimity, almost with desire, since she has fulfilled her purpose.

A third type of violence leading to death is related in *Le Gueux*, where Cloche, a crippled and hapless beggar, is beaten and kicked almost to death by the local villagers, after he has been caught killing one of their chickens in an effort to save himself from starvation:

'Les gens de la ferme arrivaient à leur tour qui se mirent avec le patron à assommer le mendiant. Puis, quand ils furent las de le battre, ils le ramassèrent et l'emportèrent, et l'enfermèrent.'

Cloche has survived for forty years by begging around the houses in the area. As time has elapsed, so the villagers have proven less receptive to his requests for sustenance:

'Dans les villages, on ne lui donnait guère: on le connaissait trop; on était fatigué de lui depuis quarante ans qu'on le voyait promener de masure en masure son corps loque-teux et difforme sur ses deux pattes de bois.'

Eventually, no one is prepared to sustain him any longer:

'Depuis deux jours, il n'avait point mangé. Personne ne lui donnait plus rien. On ne voulait plus de lui à la fin.'

But there is more to it than the eventual rejection of his small demands. Maupassant's insistent description of his tattered and deformed body, suggests that he is outlawed as much for his freakishness as for his begging. This is further taken up in the aggressive language the villagers adopt towards him:

'Pourquoi qu' tu n' va point dans l's autes villages, au lieu de béquiller toujours par ci?'

Thus, the violence inflicted on Cloche is not simply the most final and easily recognizable form, which ends with his being beaten near to death. It is also the violence of rejection and exclusion. When the women on the doorsteps comment:

'On n'peut purtant pas nourrir ce fainéant toute l'année',

this is as much a form of aggressive behaviour towards a weak and needy human being as any physical beating. It is, after all, abundantly clear from his physical disability, that Cloche is in no position to fend for himself in a hard winter. When he is eventually marched off half-dead to his confinement, the insults hurled at him are no less a form of violent behaviour than the villagers' fists and feet.

His rejection by the local people leads albeit unintentionally to his starvation in prison:

'On l'enferma dans la prison du bourg. Les gendarmes ne pensèrent pas qu'il pouvait avoir besoin de manger, et on le laissa jusqu'au lendemain',

which event is a logical consequence of the behaviour to which he has been previously subjected. Little wonder that, for once, Maupassant should feel moved to comment in a most direct fashion:

'Mais, quand on vint pour l'interroger au petit matin, on le trouva mort, sur le sol. Quelle surprise!'

Whether Cloche's death is finally occasioned by his beating or his hunger, is deliberately left open, since both are part of what is essentially the same process. There are forms of violence to the person which are not seen and which do not show on the body as bruises, burning, or bullet-holes. Equally destructive and equally violent, though not so rapid, may be years of rejection and lack of compassion.

What we may term the violence of selfishness is seen in *Pierrot*, a superficially amusing tale, in which Mme. Lefèvre's dog is eventually left to starve in a pit, because his mistress is not prepared to feed both him and another, stronger, abandoned dog. The latter takes for itself the food brought by Mme. Lefèvre and her servant for their own animal. Parsimony proves to be a far stronger emotion than any affection for Pierrot:

'Et, suffoquée à l'idée de tous ces chiens vivant à ses dépens, elle s'en alla, emportant même ce qui restait du pain qu'elle se mit à manger en marchant.'

Once more, Maupassant is making a point which is straightforward enough. There was really no good reason why the Lefèvre dog should be abandoned in the first place, other than his owner's objection to paying a licence-fee for him. Throughout this deceptively simple tale, Mme. Lefèvre is motivated to action by stinginess. Not once do we see an important action instigated by a genuine impulse of consideration for her dog. Always, when she is faced with a crucial situation, she allows the politics of the purse to decide, with a singular lack of real compassion.

Affection and compassion for Pierrot last only as long as it suits Mme. Lefèvre's pocket, after which the reader witnesses a rejection not wholly dissimilar to that suffered by Cloche:

'la faim les presse; ils s'attaquent, luttent longtemps, acharnés; et le plus fort mange le plus faible, le dévore vivant.'

The old woman's deliberations are humorous in an ironic way, and a mock epic tone is sometimes employed by Maupassant, so that the reader should not become too involved in the story, but events underline Lefèvre's lack of real affection for the world.

The violence of rejection in another form is a leit-motif in Maupassant's masterpiece, *Boule de suif*. The author shows how the girl of the title, a *fille de joie*, surrenders what she and the reader would regard as her honour to a Prussian officer in order that her coach companions and herself may be freed from the temporary captivity under which he has placed them. Predictably, once she has succumbed, she is abandoned by her fellow travellers:

> 'Personne ne la regardait, ne songeait à elle. Elle se sentait noyée dans le mépris de ces gredins honnêtes qui l'avaient sacrifiée d'abord, rejetée ensuite, comme une chose malpropre et inutile.'

In this case, Maupassant demonstrates how the moral blackmail exerted upon her is nothing other than psychological violence, inflicted to satisfy the ends of self-seeking people. The count, for example, uses all the pressure of his exalted position to force her into action:

> 'Il lui parla de ce ton familier, paternel, un peu dédaigneux, que les hommes posés emploient avec les filles, l'appelant "ma chère enfant", la traitant du haut de sa position sociale, de son honorabilité indiscutée.'

Maupassant delves beneath the surface of behaviour to present human violence as more than single acts of physical aggression. It is seen to be as much the contemptuous dismissal of disadvantaged or otherwise weaker individuals, human or animal, or the simple process of ignoring them and their needs. Man would appear to cooperate socially, but only insofar as it suits his aggressive psyche, which has been given him by an amoral and impersonal Providence. Those who are not strong enough to have bargaining strength or to survive the life process are worn-out and eventually destroyed by it.

Questions on Authors

ALAIN-FOURNIER

1 Why should *Le Grand Meaulnes* be so widely read by both children and adults?

2 Discuss the view that more than anything else, *Le Grand Meaulnes* is a novel about unhappiness.

3 Analyse the elements which make *Le Grand Meaulnes* a unique novel.

4 Which are the elements employed by Alain-Fournier to create atmosphere in *Le Grand Meaulnes*?

5 What makes *Le Grand Meaulnes* such an ambiguous novel?

6 How much of *Le Grand Meaulnes* is dream and how much reality?

7 To what extent would you agree with the statement that if *Le Grand Meaulnes* has a hero at all, it is François, not Augustin?

8 In what ways may *Le Grand Meaulnes* be said to be a fusion of *notations réalistes et une poésie née de l'expérience intérieure?*

9 *Le héros de mon livre est un homme dont l'enfance fut trop belle.* Discuss.

ANOUILH

1 How faithful is Anouilh to classical myth in *Antigone*?

2 How does Anouilh deal with historical fact in *L'Alouette*?

3 From your reading of any of Anouilh's plays, how far may his work be regarded as essentially pessimistic?

4 Discuss the view that Anouilh's abiding preoccupation in his plays is with revolt.

5 Discuss the similarities between Anouilh and Giraudoux as dramatists.

6 *Dans l'univers d'Anouilh s'affrontent deux sortes d'êtres; d'un côté les êtres vulgaires... de l'autre, les 'gens de la bonne race'.* Discuss.

7 *Le théâtre d'Anouilh est animé d'une conviction pathétique.* What are the implications of this statement?

APOLLINAIRE

1 In what sense may Apollinaire be termed a *modernist*?

2 What evidence have you encountered in your reading of Apollinaire which indicates that he was hostile to tradition?

3 Examine the technical innovations which Apollinaire introduced into his work.

4 How unfair would be the criticism that there was little more to Apollinaire than technique?

5 *Guillaume Apollinaire est peut-être le plus cosmopolite des poètes français.* Discuss.

6 *Puis lentement je m'en allai pour quêter la Rose du Monde.* How far did Apollinaire succeed in his quest?

BALZAC

1 In what sense may Balzac's novels be referred to as *documentary*?

2 Assess Balzac as a creator of character.

3 Discuss the view that Balzac's novels are so full of colour that they are near to distorting reality.

4 What characteristics of Romanticism do you discern in the work of Honoré de Balzac?

5 *Les femmes ne sont pas plus les dupes des comédies que jouent les hommes que des leurs.* Analyse Balzac's female characters in the light of his own comment.

BAUDELAIRE

1 To what extent is Baudelaire's poetry helped by his painful sense of honesty?

2 In what ways may Baudelaire be termed the poet of the modern city?

3 Give reasons for Baudelaire's sustained popularity as a poet. How valid is Baudelaire's claim to be a genius among poets?

5 Why is Baudelaire's poetry often preferred by modern readers to that of the main Romantics?

6 *Hypocrite lecteur!* What are the qualities in Baudelaire's work which allow him to insult his readership, while retaining their affection?

7 *Soyez béni, mon Dieu, qui donnez la souffrance*
Comme un divin remède à nos impuretés –
What precisely do critics mean when they refer to Baudelaire's satanism?

BECKETT

1 In what sense may Beckett's plays be termed *absurd*?

2 From your reading of Beckett's plays, comment on his view of language as something irrational.

3 How far do you agree with the assessment that Beckett's characters are scarcely human?

4 *En français c'est plus facile d'écrire sans style.* In what measure does Beckett's own comment help us to understand the implications of his French plays?

5 *Je voudrais te poser quelques simples questions... Je ne connais pas de réponses.* Analyse any major play(s) by Beckett in the light of this quotation.

BOSCO

1 Discuss the view that there is more to Bosco's works than simple description of life in Provence.

2 What are the dominant themes in the work of Bosco?

3 What part does Nature play in Bosco's work?

4 On what do you feel Bosco's reputation as a novelist rests?

5 *Le temps s'enfonce dans l'absence; et les heures nous quittent sans secousse.* What significance does this quotation from *Malicroix* have for Bosco's work as a whole?

CAMUS

1 What does Camus find *absurd* in *L'Étranger*?

2 What is there in Camus' work which makes him a source of inspiration for so many people?

3 To what extent may *La Peste* be called an allegorical novel?

4 From your reading of *L'Exil et le royaume*, what justification is there for referring to Camus as a *committed* writer?

5 To what extent is Camus' view of the human condition pessimistic?

6 From your reading of Camus' work, why should he have become such a cult figure for the youth of his time?

7 Examine the significance of any of Camus' major works as a comment on life and society.

8 *Mon royaume tout entier est de ce monde.* Analyse any work of Camus in the light of this self-appraisal.

9 *Si la seule solution est la mort, nous ne sommes pas sur la bonne voie.* How far may this statement by Camus be taken as an epitaph both for him and his work?

CESBRON

1 In what ways may Cesbron be said to be a *committed* writer?

2 What picture does *Les Saints vont en enfer* present of the workers' Paris?

3 Analyse the progression in Étienne's character through the various stages of *Les Saints vont en enfer.*

4 *Voici un livre qui risque de déplaire un peu partout.* Examine any major work by Cesbron in the light of this comment.

5 *On chercherait en vain Sagny sur une carte; mais ce que j'en raconte, on le trouvera dans presque toute la banlieue de Paris.* How valid is Cesbron's comment?

COCTEAU

1 How far do you agree with the opinion that Cocteau destroyed a good legend in *La Machine infernale* and left nothing in its place?

2 In what sense may Cocteau be regarded as *avant-garde?*

3 Examine the function and importance of dramatic irony in *La Machine infernale.*

4 How does Cocteau adapt the classical myth in *La Machine infernale?*

5 Comment on the structure of *La Machine infernale* and of the devices used by Cocteau to maintain the interest of the audience.

6 *La carrière théâtrale de Jean Cocteau est celle d'un Protée, merveilleusement attentif à devenir la mode du lendemain.* Discuss with reference to any of Cocteau's major works.

COLETTE

1 To what extent is *Le Blé en herbe* a re-working of Colette's own youth?

2 Identify the elements in Colette's work which suggest that she is much more than merely a competent writer.

3 How far is *Le Blé en herbe* a convincing portrayal of young love?

4 Until quite recently, eminent literati were still describing Colette as *merely a feminist.* What had they missed?

5 Discuss the view that there is much more to Colette's writing than sheer sensuality.

6 In what measure may Colette's novels be described as having a structure which is loosely-knit and a style which is impressionistic?

7 *Il faut soigner cet enfant... Ne peut-on sauver cette femme?* What autobiographical chord is struck by this line from Colette's *La Maison de Claudine?*

DE BEAUVOIR

1 Analyse the relationship between de Beauvoir and her father, as it appears in *Mémoires d'une jeune fille rangée.*

2 From your reading of Simone de Beauvoir, how did her religious upbringing influence both her adolescence and her literary output?

3 What evidence is there from your reading of Simone de Beauvoir that she is above all an analytical writer?

4 *Féministe convaincue, Simone de Beauvoir n'a cessé de militer pour que les femmes aient une vie indépendante.* What are the other qualities in de Beauvoir's work which make her a worthwhile author?

5 *Une des raisons de ma pruderie, c'était sans doute ce dégoût mêlé de frayeur que le mâle inspire ordinairement aux vierges.* Analyse *Mémoires d'une jeune fille rangée* in the light of this comment.

DE MONTHERLANT

1 What evidence is there to support the claim that de Montherlant is basically a misogynist?

2 Why should a work like *Jeunes Filles* arouse such passions?

3 How far do you support the comment that Montherlant should have carried on playing football and left literature to those who know about it?

4 *Montherlant oscille entre un jansénisme sportif et un hédonisme où refleurit la sagesse d'Omar Khayyam.* Discuss.

5 *À la fois un moraliste, c'est-à-dire celui qui étudie les passions, et un moralisateur, c'est-à-dire celui qui propose une certaine morale.* Analyse any of the works of Henri de Montherlant in the light of this quotation.

DURAS

1 Examine the significance of the dialogue in *Moderato Cantabile.*

2 From your reading of *Moderato Cantabile*, analyse the hallmarks of Duras' style.

3 To what extent is Anne Desbaresdes an autobiographical character?

4 Analyse the forces preventing a successful union between Anne and Chauvin in *Moderato Cantabile.*

5 What did Duras mean, when she said that *Moderato Cantabile* had allowed her to achieve *une écriture corporelle*?

FLAUBERT

1 What is Flaubert's attitude to the title character in *Madame Bovary*?

2 Analyse the structure of *Madame Bovary* or *L'Éducation sentimentale*.

3 In what ways could *Madame Bovary* be said to have made the realist novel respectable?

4 Discuss Flaubert's use of irony in any one of his major novels.

5 Assess any of Flaubert's major novels as a morbid and impersonal study in disillusionment.

6 *Madame Bovary est essentiellement une tragédie bourgeoise de l'illusion.* Interpret this comment on Flaubert's major novel.

7 *Pour bien comprendre Flaubert, il faut le mettre au-dessus et en dehors des écoles, des idées et des formules d'écoles.* Discuss.

ANATOLE FRANCE

1 From your reading of any of Anatole France's novels, provide an assessment of his narrative art.

2 How far does Anatole France succeed in providing credible female characters in his work?

3 To what extent could *Les Dieux ont soif* be regarded as a *rationalist* novel?

4 Why should Anatole France have been compared so often with Voltaire?

5 Why do you think that Anatole France should have been hailed as a great writer, only to languish almost unread for the next half century?

6 *Le Paris de la révolution, et particulièrement de la Terreur, y revit non seulement dans son atmosphère historique mais dans son existence quotidienne.* How far do you agree with this comment on *Les Dieux ont soif*?
   In what sense may *L'Île des Pingouins* be referred to as *une allégorie bouffonne*?

FROMENTIN

1 How difficult is it to separate autobiography and fiction in *Dominique*?

2 What are the qualities in *Dominique* which suggest it was written by a painter?

3 *Dominique? Ce n'est qu'un petit roman trop personnel.* In your opinion, how just or unjust is this comment on Fromentin's novel?

4 *Une oeuvre délicate qui traverse la patrie des sentiments.* Discuss with reference to *Dominique*.

GIDE

1 Analyse the contrast between profane love and pure religion in *La Symphonie pastorale*.

2 What evidence is there of the *communist-bandwaggon effect* in Gide's novels of the period?

3 Comment on the structure of *La Symphonie pastorale*.

4 Examine the significance of the theme of blindness in *La Symphonie pastorale*.

5 From your reading of Gide, in what sense can he be said to be a moralist?

6 Examine Gide's conception of *disponibilité* as exemplified in any of his major works.

7 Analyse the concept of the *acte gratuit* as set-out in *Les Caves du Vatican*.

8 Discuss the view that *Les Caves du Vatican* is little more than a scurrilous lampoon.

9 *Familles, je vous hais!* What evidence of Gide's famous cry of revolt have you found in his novels?

GIRAUDOUX

1 Examine Giraudoux's treatment of the theme of *le couple parfait* in his work.

2 Comment on Giraudoux's predilection for classical myth/biblical history in his plays.

3 How far would you agree that *La Guerre de Troie n'aura pas lieu* is a play of universal implications?

4 What is meant by the term *mauvaise foi* in the context of Giraudoux's work?

5 To what extent do you agree with the statement that *Hélène* in *La Guerre de Troie n'aura pas lieu* is an essentially inaccessible character?

6 *Le style, ce secret dont l'écrivain est le seul dépositaire.* What is so unique about the style of Jean Giraudoux?

7 In what sense may *La Guerre de Troie n'aura pas lieu* be said to be *un drame poignant, le cri d'une conscience moderne en révolte*?

8 *La forme du dialogue est, dans l'état actuel de l'esprit humain, la seule qui, selon moi, puisse convenir à l'exposition des idées philosophiques.* How relevant is Renan's statement on his own work to that of Giraudoux?

LOTI

1 To what extent are Loti's novels a re-working of his own experience?

2 How far do you agree that *Pêcheur d'Islande* shows Loti to have a profound understanding both of the sea and of ordinary people?

3 How far would it be true to say that Loti presents a romanticized view of life in Brittany in *Pêcheur d'Islande*?

4 What picture does *Pêcheur d'Islande* present of life in Brittany at the time of the novel?

5 *'Pêcheur d'Islande' n'est véritablement pas un roman.* What do you feel was in the mind of the person who made this comment?

MAUPASSANT

1 Examine the art of Maupassant as a short-story writer.

2 Analyse the major elements of Maupassant's style as a writer of *contes*.

3 From your reading of Maupassant's short stories, with which aspects of society does he appear to be especially concerned?

4 Why might Maupassant be said to present a one-sided picture of humanity?

5 How far do you subscribe to the view that Maupassant is above all an observer of the bourgeoisie and of the Norman peasantry?

6 Discuss the view that although *Boule de suif* was one of the first major novella to be written, it is unlikely ever to be surpassed.

7 *Tout d'abord il est dans la littérature le maître certain du conte, le classique du conte... par la solidité et la variété des êtres vivants qu'il pétrit dans une pâte de peinture...* Discuss with reference to Maupassant's *contes*.

MAURIAC

1 Discuss the view that Mauriac writes to solve the problems of his own conscience.

2 What importance does Mauriac attach to structure in (any of) his major novels?

3 From your reading of Mauriac, to what extent do you incline to the view that he sees the family as the prime source of conflict?

4 What evidence is there for the view that Mauriac's main characters show him to be obsessed with sinners?

5 Examine the attitudes to money and property implicit in any one of Mauriac's major novels.

6 In *Thérèse Desqueyroux*, how far do Mauriac's sympathies lie with his main character?

7 *Thérèse Desqueyroux est probablement le plus représentatif de mes romans....* Do you agree with Mauriac's judgement on his novel?

8 *La société veut une condamnation: la société, qu'est-ce donc, sinon l'ensemble des familles?* Analyse any of Mauriac's major novels in the light of this comment.

MOLIÈRE

1 Discuss *Le Misanthrope* as a study in hypocrisy.

2 Why may *Le Misanthrope* be said to be a delicately balanced play?

3 How much more is *Les Femmes savantes* than pure social comedy?

4 How and for what reasons does Molière make preciosity a subject for comedy?

5 Why should *Le Tartuffe* have originally been all but banned for five years?

6 In what respects may *Le Tartuffe* and *Don Juan* both be said to be provocative plays?

7 What are the satirical implications of *Don Juan*?

8 What is meant by the term *l'esprit gaulois*, when applied to Molière?

9 *Aujourd'hui, un auteur attaqué se défendrait en écrivant dans les journaux... Molière, comédien avant tout, aimait s'adresser directement à son public.* Analyse the implications of this comment for any of Molière's more controversial plays.

PAGNOL

1 Why do Pagnol's plays have such potential for the cinema?

2 Analyse the character and attitudes of Marcel's father in *Le Château de ma mère*.

3 Why may *Topaze* reasonably be described as a relatively conventional comedy?

4 Discuss the view that Pagnol's film *La Femme du boulanger* justified his decision to abandon the theatre.

5 *Pagnol peignait une galérie de personnages sommaires mais sympathiques.* Discuss.

PROUST

1 How far is it possible to separate Marcel, the narrator of *Du Côté de chez Swann*, from Marcel Proust, the writer?

2 Show how Proust combines nostalgia with acute observation of weakness.

3 Discuss Proust's use of humour in *Du Côté de chez Swann*.

4 To what extent do you agree with the view that Proust's work implies lasting happiness to be impossible?

5 Assess the value of Proust's work as a social documentary.

6 *Proust est quelqu'un dont le regard est infiniment plus subtil et plus attentif que le nôtre, et qui nous prête ce regard, tout le temps que nous le lisons.* Discuss.

7 *Proust étudie sentiments et caractères avec une telle acuité.* Discuss.

ROLLAND

1 In what ways may Rolland be termed an *anti-rationalist*?

2 How far does Rolland's strong humanitarianism shine through in his work?

3 What do you think was meant by the critic who described Rolland as *un humaniste tolstoïen*?

4 *Romain Rolland a prouvé qu'une grande construction romanesque n'était pas obligatoirement soumise à la formule flaubertienne.* Discuss.

SARTRE

1 For what reasons is *La Nausée* often considered not to be a *proper* novel?

2 From your reading of any of Sartre's major works, what do you understand by the term *existentialism*?

3 How much truth is there in the statement that in both Sartre's novels and plays, his characters are simply vehicles for his philosophical argument?

4 What does *Les Mains sales* reveal to us of Sartre's own political attitudes?

5 Discuss the view that in Sartre's major plays he allows metaphysics to intrude to the detriment of character and plot.

6 How much of Sartre himself has been put into the character of Étienne in *Les Chemins de la liberté*?

7 *C'est dans les livres que j'ai rencontré l'univers* is one of Sartre's many well-known statements about himself. What exactly do *we* encounter in his novels?

8 *Quand une fois la liberté a explosé dans une âme d'homme, les dieux ne peuvent plus rien contre cet homme-là.* What justification is there for seeing in these lines a *leit-motif* running through the whole of Sartre's literary output?

STENDHAL

1 To what extent may Stendhal's novels be described as *precise*?

2 How far is *Le Rouge et le Noir* a political novel?

3 How successful is Stendhal as a creator of character?

4 Do you agree with the view that Stendhal's characters are more psychological studies than flesh and blood?

5 In what ways may Stendhal be described as a subjective novelist?

6 To what purpose and effect does Stendhal employ irony in his novels?

7 *C'était la destinée de Napoléon, serait-ce un jour la sienne?* Examine the significance of the Napoléon motif in *Le Rouge et le Noir*.

8 *Pour Julien, faire fortune, c'était d'abord sortir de Verrières; il abhorrait sa patrie. Tout ce qu'il y voyait glaçait son imagination.* Examine *Le Rouge et le Noir* in the light of the above quotation.

TROYAT

1 To what extent do you agree with the statement that Troyat's novels suffer from too much psycho-analysis?

2 Analyse the view that Troyat's novels are deceptively straightforward.

3 Assess *La Tête sur les épaules* as a study of an adolescent undergoing a crisis of awareness.

4 Is there any truth in the statement that Troyat's novels are not helped by their endings?

5 *Le roman est, pour moi, une entreprise artistique destinée à rendre ce qui aurait pu être plausible, aussi émouvant que ce qui est.* Discuss this comment by Troyat in relation to any of his major novels.

6 *Je revendique le privilège singulier de n'être qu'un monsieur qui aime raconter des histoires.* In your opinion, how fair has Troyat been in this self-assessment?

VALLÈS

1 How much of Vallès' own past history do we discern from a reading of his work?

2 Discuss the view that Vallès' work is hampered by the intolerant excesses of his political convictions.

3 How far would you agree that the major feeling one gains from reading Vallès is of a man at odds with the age in which he lived?

4 *La bohème et l'anarchie composaient son univers.* Discuss this comment on Vallès.

VOLTAIRE

1 For what reasons is *Candide* still read today?

2 Analyse Voltaire's use of irony in *Candide*.

3 Discuss the view that *Candide* is much more than a *conte philosophique*.

4 How far do you agree with the view that in our age little has changed from the times of *Candide*, except for the nature of the disasters?

5 *If for nothing else, 'Candide' would be remembered as a plea for tolerance.* Discuss.

6 *Mais que pourrait Voltaire aujourd'hui?* Why should such a question be asked? Base your answer on your study of *Candide*.

7 *Candide, oeuvre désespérée et désespérante – ou tonique, joyeuse, féconde?* What is *your* reaction to Voltaire's most famous work?

ZOLA

1 What in your opinion are the features which make *Germinal* a great novel?

2 In what ways may Zola's novels be referred to as *determinist?*

3 Discuss the view that Zola's main characters are little more than symbols.

4 Examine the importance of structure in any one or two of Zola's major novels.

5 In what sense may *La Fortune des Rougon* be described as a documentary novel?

6 Assess the impact made by *Germinal* on the French middle-class readership of the day.

7 *Zola a voulu montrer ce qu'étaient face au bien-être des bourgeois, la condition misérable des mineurs et leur travail éreintant.* How far is *Germinal* successful in achieving Zola's aims?

8 *Bien qu'il ait abordé avec justesse et clairvoyance, certains des mécanismes de la société moderne, Zola ne donne pas le premier rang aux questions économiques.* To what extent do you agree or disagree with this statement?

GENERAL POETRY

1 Discuss either Lamartine or Musset as a Romantic poet.

2 What are the fundamental features of de Vigny's poetry?

3 Examine Lamartine as an elegiac poet.

4 How far do you agree with the opinion that if you take away the music from Verlaine's poetry, there is not much left?

5 Examine the theme of nostalgia, as evident in Verlaine's poetry.

6 Analyse the statement that the youthfulness of Rimbaud's poetry gives it its strength as well as its weakness.

7 Why should an apparent anachronism like Leconte de Lisle be once more favoured by the poetry-reading public?

8 Comment on the aggression in Laforgue's poetry.

9 Analyse the linguistic innovations in the poetry of Laforgue.

10 Examine the lyricism of Lamartine's verse.

11 Discuss the view that Vian is the poet of the modern man.

12 Trace the iconoclasm in Boris Vian's poetry.

13 Show the strength of Prévert's visual imagination in the *Paroles*.

14 Comment on Verlaine's mastery of poetic techniques.

15 What was there in Hugo's poetry that should have made him such a model for young, rising poets like Charles Baudelaire?

THE CINEMA

1 How much truth is there in the statement that Jean Renoir left little for succeeding film-makers to accomplish?

2 Examine the effect of the American thriller on the French cinema of the past twenty-five years.

3 Discuss the view that the French cinema was ruined by the advent of colour.

4 Describe Truffaut's use of colour.

5 Why should reaction to the films of Godard be so polarized?

6 Compare and contrast the films of Godard and Truffaut.

7 In what ways may Jean Renoir and Gabin be said to represent the uniqueness of the French cinema?

8 Assess the contribution of Montand, Belmondo and Delon *or* Signoret, Moreau and Anouk Aimée to the French cinema.

9 Discuss the view that the quality of the French cinema has been adversely affected by the success of television.

10 Give an assessment of the movement known as the *nouvelle vague*.

11 What do you understand by the term *cinéma-vérité*? Illustrate your answer by reference to at least three film-makers.

12 Assess the contribution of Jacques Tati to the cinema.

13 Give a critical analysis of any French film you have seen recently.

14 Write notes on *three* of the following:

Robert Bresson; Marguerite Duras; Éric Rohmer; Pierre Étaix; Claude Lelouche; Alain Robbe-Grillet; Alain Resnais.

15 Provide an assessment of the contemporary French cinema.

16 How far is it true to say that the new, young French film-makers do not compare with those of the 1960s and '70s?

GENERAL QUESTIONS

1 Assess the contribution to society of any French-speaking painter, musician or architect.

2 Write notes on *three* of the following: Renoir, Debussy, Gauguin, Picasso, Milhaud, Le Corbusier, Dali.

3 Discuss the role of Marshal Pétain in Second World War France.

4 Give a brief description of the Surrealist movement.

5 Assess the significance of the Dreyfus affair.

6 Examine the legacy of the French colonization of one of the following:

Algeria/Indo-China/Morocco/Tunisia.

7 Discuss Bergson's view of intelligence.

8 Analyse the contribution of Bergson, Marie Curie or Pasteur to Western society.

9 In what sense has Provence not lost its artistic legacy?

10 Describe the work and achievements of Jean Monnet.

11 Assess Émile Durkheim's contribution to sociology.

12 Trace the history of the French working man during this century.

13 How have modern means of transport affected French life during the course of this century?

14 How are the French adjusting to an era of unemployment?

15 How has life in France been affected by membership of the EEC?

BACKGROUND QUESTIONS

1 What picture does any French novel you have read present of French society in the twentieth century?

2 What have you learnt of nineteenth-century social problems from any work of French literature relating to that period?

3 If you have read a work by an *écrivain engagé* what comment does he or she make on modern society within its framework?

4 If any of your set texts was written in or near the period of the Second World War, to what extent does it reflect contemporary cares and considerations?

5 If you have read a work in which real people are presented in fictionalized form, assess whether the work has enabled you to understand them and their times.

6 To what extent is the prevailing Establishment approved or criticized in any of the French works you have read?

7 How far does any of your set texts help you towards an understanding of the period in which it is set?

8 If you have read a French text set in the provinces, assess the picture it presents of provincial life.

A Glossary of Literary Terms

The Absurd (*the literature of the*) is characterized by a strong sense of the irrational nature of our experience of the world, often combined with an intense awareness of our solitary nature and of the finality of our eventual death.

The Avant-Garde is an artistic phenomenon, which underlines the close inter-relationship between the Arts. It is a movement which was most evident in the early, optimistic years of this century. *Modernism*, as it was often called, embraced fauvism and cubism in painting, the poetry of writers such as Apollinaire and Jacob and the theatre of Alfred Jarry. Whatever the medium, art that is avant-garde attempts to investigate, assess and understand all that is new and worth knowing in the worlds of science and ideas.

Classicism was a period in French literature and thought covering the seventeenth and early eighteenth centuries, during which the main strands of literary endeavour – drama, poetry and prose works – were evolving out of the strictures of the immediate Post-Renaissance. However, Classicism eventually developed its own strict conventions, underlying which was the belief that perfection in literature had already been achieved in the classical cultures of Greece and Rome, which were to be used as a model.

Dadaism was a brief but influential movement which arose as a reaction to the ordered futility of the First World War. It laid great stress on instinct, especially in self-expression, where words, individual or grouped, were consequently felt capable of every or of no significance, according to the whim of the user.

Engagement (*commitment*) is an act of will on the part of the individual, committing him or her to a positive and practical involvement in human society. The *écrivain engagé* thus writes out of a strong sense of involvement in the concerns of his or her fellows.

Existentialism is the doctrine that the individual human being's existence is given meaning and justification by his or her positive actions and commitment (*engagement* q.v.). Such commitment often implies a high degree of social and/or political involvement in society.

Naturalism was the late nineteenth-century literary movement based on the doctrine that the writer's art should combine the faithful observation and reproduction of nature with a form of scientific method. Hence, characters within a work are seen to be the product of their own heredity and environment.

The New Novel is a modern reaction to the traditional novel, especially as exemplified in the nineteenth century. *New novelists* such as Butor, Robbe-Grillet and Simon, reject the neat, cohesive nature of such earlier works as inappropriate to the second half of the twentieth century. Instead, they experiment with devices such as the use of interchangeable chapters, the introduction of deliberate ambiguities and inconsistencies, changes in the dimensions of time and place. It is hardly surprising that the *New Novelists* tend to be regarded as obsessed with technique.

Parnassianism was essentially a poetic movement, which, employing historical, classical and exotic subject matter, set itself standards of perfection in form and content, which were only to be attained through the application of a highly disciplined and impersonal poetic style.

Rationalism was particularly significant in the first half of the eighteenth century. It was characterized by a movement away from fictionalized, imaginative writing towards the literature of ideas, covering the whole range of contemporary economic, philosophical, political, religious and social themes.

Realism arose as a reaction to *Romanticism* (q.v.), out of a belief that Art should be a sincere and true reflection of reality. Life was to be reproduced with meticulous accuracy and there was a consequent strong dislike of such devices as exaggeration, idealization, extreme coincidence. *Naturalism* (q.v.) is an extreme development of Realism.

Revolt (the literature of) is a general term applied to part or all of the work of many twentieth-century authors. Despite their different media and the disparity in their themes and personal styles, writers such as Beckett, Camus, Genet, Ionesco, Sartre, show a rejection of the easy values of an optimistic existence. For reasons discussed under *existentialism* (q.v.) and the *Absurd* (q.v.), they write as a form of revolt against such a system for living and use devices to jolt us out of our comfortable acceptance of things as they apparently are.

Romanticism is a movement which first arose as a reaction to the excessive realism. The senses and the emotions play a dominant role, as does Nature, in which our drives and our fluctuating states of mind are reflected. There is also an emphasis on artistic freedom and the writer's need to communicate his deepest thoughts.

Surrealism was an artistic and literary movement of the 1920s and '30s which reacted against the violent and absurd nature of society by producing art which was itself violent, absurd and dream-like, reflecting in particular the influence of Freud's theory of dreams.

Symbolism was an artistic and poetic movement characterized by a movement away from concrete description and towards the creation of impressions and sensations. These symbolized the feelings and the state of mind of the artist and stressed the basic symbolic relationship between sounds, scents and colours.

APPENDIX 4

Answers to Assignments

Ch. 2, page 19
    (a) 1-lyrical   b) 3-popular   c) 1-pathos   d) 2-terse   e) 4-committed   f) 2-pessimistic   g) 4-optimism for   h) 1-dense   i) 2-ironic   j) 4-ironic.

Ch. 9, page 74   1d   2c   3b   4a   5e
    page 75   A1   B4   C1   D4   E2

Ch. 13, *page 101: Spelling*
    (a) correspondence   (b) accommodation, purposes   (c) practise
    (d) preceded, pursue, unattainable   (e) vocabulary, descriptive   (f) perturbed, relevance   (g) friends, perceive, priest's, conceit   (h) development, relatively, successful   (i) fulfils, role   (j) scarcely, subsistence   (k) definite, obsession

Ch. 13, page 102: Vague expression and bad syntax (suggested alternatives)
    (a) This is another example of the difficulties to be found in Sartre's work.
    (b) The author examines the question of personal relations, which he sees as underlying our behaviour.
    (c) Chamson is a modern author, with the modern author's determination to present problems as he sees them.
    (d) There is a completeness about Baudelaire's work.
    (e) The two works provide a balance.
    (f) Thanks to Pagnol's lightness of touch, his plays are easy to understand.
    (g) A tall, handsome schoolboy, he lives alone with his mother in Paris.
    (h) It is not surprising, when one takes his spiritual development into account.
    (i) Light is another quality used by Fournier to create an element of mystery.
    (j) The fact that the author does not stipulate whether she is 'une femme ou une jeune fille' helps to retain this element of suspense.
    (k) To a largely catholic population, the mother figure would be something very sacred.

Ch. 13, page 102: Popular and slang expression (suggested alternatives)
    (a) One must be careful not to miss happiness, unlike those in the novel.
    (b) This is much more realistic than a surprise ending, promising fairy-tale happiness.
    (c) The story has a dramatic beginning.

   (d) The father's irrational behaviour had further consequences.

   (e) The maid is unable to put up with such behaviour from her master.

   (f) The reader is bound to agree with the point Vailland is making.

   (g) The discovery fascinates him.

   (h) He decides to obtain his revenge.

   (i) Again, Marise is hurt by one of life's ironies.

   (j) She is in a highly emotional state.

   (k) The ending is so obvious as to have little effect.

   (l) Gaston, socially ill at ease, does not know quite what he should do or say.

   (m) Bazin's picture of the woman is a horrifying one.

   (n) It is a question of self-preservation/It is a matter of self-interest.

   (o) The battle is at its zenith by this stage.

Ch. 13, page 103: Cliché (suggested possible alternatives)

   (a) During her absence, he describes himself as isolated.

   (b) He is a bewildered youth, deprived of affection.

   (c) Money is seen to be the motivation behind the evil behaviour in this play.

   (d) By keeping them apart, he weakens and overcomes their defences.

   (e) When he murders his wife and blames it on Serge, he achieves a double purpose.

   (f) Isaïe does not know what to do without his brother, Marcellin.

   (g) The author has the ability to let her readers see the landscapes she describes.

   (h) The novel ends on an optimistic note, with the suggestion that the three will live in harmony.

   (i) We always have the impression that Bernard depends on her to think and act for him.

Ch. 13, page 103: Involved writing

   (a) This conception could easily be valid, as there is a fragmented quality about the action. Always, happiness seems to be threatened or disrupted by some external danger, of which the most obvious example is the mishap at the wedding party.

   (b) Perhaps it is one's definition of happiness which decides the answer. Given the dream-like quality of the novel, happiness does appear to be an illusion. Out of this illusion, not one of the principal characters obtains lasting happiness. Surely, this is much more realistic than a highly optimistic conclusion, where the couples depart, enveloped in the roseate glow of the setting sun?

   (c) To me, they appear content with what they have, up to a point, but they are also aware of what they have missed. This is especially true of Xavier, who seems to note and understand the situation more than anyone, but is powerless to impose. Even in the case of Christian and Yveline's elopement, his efforts achieve nothing, since he has neither sufficient influence nor persuasiveness.

   (d) Whether or not the ending of the work may be said to be optimistic depends upon whether the final events have been accurately reported and are to be seen as conclusive, or whether there is the implication that they are a further stage in a continuing process towards the light.

Ch. 13, page 104: Repetition (suggested possible alternatives)
  (a) Maupassant uses as little description as possible in his stories. Its purpose is to provide background.
  (b) He thinks over possible alternatives, such as considering himself someone else's son.
  (c) This idea concludes a certain line of thought.
  (d) Such a power is a dominant quality, since this situation can alter as a consequence of the family's efforts.
  (e) She perceives the problem, thinks it through, then resolves to act and takes it to its logical conclusion.
  (f) We are clearly left with a definitive statement.
  (g) Given that this is true, I suppose we should accept the situation.
  (h) This is the first occasion for us to be presented with the author's theory of time.
  (i) It is at this point that his real and obsessive hatred of his mother begins to reach a new level of intensity.

Ch. 13, page 104: Over-verbalization (suggested possible alternatives)
  (a) In terms of the *conte philosophique*, Voltaire may be regarded as a master of style, because of his ability to use effectively, all of the literary devices available to him.
  (b) The author stands outside of society so that he may observe it as it comes near to destroying itself, through its lack of common purpose.
  (c) The above statement may be regarded as a model of validity, with its acute observation.
  (d) Description is an essential element of this fictionalized account, because of the realism it brings.
  (e) To soften our reaction, the author introduces side-issues and comments.
  (f) The contrast, so near the surface, which exists between the two children of the family, is never far from the reader's mind.
  (g) It is indeed the hub of the action, on which plot and character turn.
  (h) Dare one sense a spark of optimism in this mutually-dependent relationship?

Ch. 13, page 104: Grammatical inaccuracy
  (a) hanged   (b) between him and her   (c) were   (d) continuous
  (e) were   (f) was   (g) ever   (h) Through her many visits, she gave hope to the convicted prisoner, languishing in prison
  (i) medium   (j) whom   (k) omit *more*   (l) won't   (m) defiance
  (n) beat   (o) drowned.